YOU, GAMES AND MARKETS

YOU, GAMES AND MARKETS

KNOW THYSELF

AS Ramasastri
A Aparajitha

PARTRIDGE

Copyright © 2023 by AS Ramasastri; A Aparajitha.

ISBN:	Hardcover	978-1-5437-0921-6
	Softcover	978-1-5437-0920-9
	eBook	978-1-5437-0919-3

All rights reserved. No part of this book may be used or reproduced by any means, graphic, electronic, or mechanical, including photocopying, recording, taping or by any information storage retrieval system without the written permission of the author except in the case of brief quotations embodied in critical articles and reviews.

Because of the dynamic nature of the Internet, any web addresses or links contained in this book may have changed since publication and may no longer be valid. The views expressed in this work are solely those of the author and do not necessarily reflect the views of the publisher, and the publisher hereby disclaims any responsibility for them.

Print information available on the last page.

To order additional copies of this book, contact
Partridge India
000 800 919 0634 (Call Free)
+91 000 80091 90634 (Outside India)
orders.india@partridgepublishing.com

www.partridgepublishing.com/india

Contents

Foreword ix
Preface xv

Chapter I: You Are What Your Emotions Are..... 1
  1. Brain and Rational Behaviour................... 2
  2. Moods and Emotions 9
  3. Emotions and Emotional Traits 11
  4. Emotional Traits and Personality 13
  5. Traits – Positive and Negative 16
  6. Negative Traits that Matter 19
  7. Can you Escape your Emotions?............ 21
  8. Caveat 26

Chapter II: Negative Traits................................ 27
  1. Anger 28
  2. Greed 34
  3. Attachment... 38
  4. Pride... 43
  5. Envy 48
  6. Fear 53
  7. Pessimism 59
  8. Quixotism 61

Chapter III: Simulated Games........................... 64
  1. Are Stock Markets Casinos? 65
  2. When you are at a Racecourse 71
  3. At the Roulette Table............................. 73

4. If you were a farmer..................78
  5. Imagine you are an angel 84
  6. To Lend or Not to 91
  7. Be Poker Faced 96
  8. Negative Traits and Behavioural Types ... 103
Chapter IV: Quantitative Methods................ 107
  1. Probability.............................. 108
  2. Random Variable.................... 122
  3. Probability Distribution 130
  4. Mean and Standard Deviation 144
  5. Correlation and Regression................... 155
  6. Random Sampling................. 163
  7. Time Series and Stochastic Processes...... 167
  8. Tying Knots........................... 175
Chapter V: Stock Market Theories 185
  1. Dow and Technical Analysis 186
  2. DuPont and Fundamental Analysis...... 194
  3. Bachelier and Random Walk Theory 206
  4. Fama and Efficient Markets
     Hypothesis 210
  5. Sharpe and the Capital Asset
     Pricing Model 215
  6. Ross and Arbitrage Pricing Theory 220
  7. Keynes and Animal Spirits................. 225
  8. Nobel Laureates and Behavioural
     Economics 230
Chapter VI: Historical Market Events 238
  1. 5Es of Asset Bubble Life Cycle............ 239

- 2. Tulip Mania (1634) 244
- 3. Vienna Stock Exchange Crash (1873) .. 247
- 4. Wall Street Crash (1929) 250
- 5. Black Monday (1987) 253
- 6. Dot-Com Burst (2000) 256
- 7. Global Financial Crisis (2008) 259
- 8. Crypto Growth 262

Chapter VII: Men and Machines : Co-Existence 263
- 1. Machines March into Markets 264
- 2. Automated Trading Systems 267
- 3. Artificial Intelligence 273
- 4. AI Based Trading Systems 280
- 5. AI and Emotions 282
- 6. AI and Ethics 285
- 7. Can you Beat an AI Based Trader? 289
- 8. Looking into the Future 293

Chapter VIII: Lessons Learnt and Way Forward 299

Recommended Reading 303

Foreword

Economists, it is said somewhat derisively, suffer from 'physics envy'. Like physicists who model the behaviour of the universe with exactitude through complex mathematical formulations, economists believed that they could model human behaviour with similar exactitude deploying similarly complex mathematical formulations. Central to this pursuit was the assumption that humans are rational, forever attempting to maximize their utility.

But that assumption does not hold. The history of economics is replete with examples of how the discipline has repeatedly been wrongfooted in predicting or explaining real world outcomes because a completely rational human being simply does not exist. Far from being cold, calculating rational machines driven entirely by self-interest, humans are – yes, just that – human. They are driven by emotions as Richard Thaler, a Nobel Prize winning economist, demonstrated in his widely acclaimed book 'Nudge', and they are driven by psychological biases as Daniel Kahneman, another Nobel Laureate, explains in his justly famous book – 'Thinking Fast and Slow'.

This book by Ramasastri, a valued colleague of mine when I was in the Reserve Bank of India (2008-13), and his daughter, Aparajitha, is grounded on that basic understanding. Drawing from their shared interest in probability theory, artificial intelligence, human behaviour and casinos, not necessarily in that order, as they are careful to add, they focus on how irrational behaviour leads people into flawed decisions in financial markets. Their endeavour is not so much to help the reader play the stock market with greater finesse, but a larger one – of helping the reader understand the roots of irrationality in herself.

That's a daunting challenge. But Ramasastri and Aparajitha approach the task with remarkable aptitude and enthusiasm pulling together concepts and ideas from a variety of disciplines and varied human experiences.

From one side, they dive deep into the psychology of emotions explaining how negative traits such as anger, greed and attachment lead our decision making astray. That would have been a scholarly endeavor if also a sterile one. But Ramasastri and Aparajitha make it remarkably engaging by explaining human emotions with examples drawn from a wide canvas stretching across time and space like Vishnusharma's Panchatantra, Homer's Iliad, Shakespeare's Macbeth, Austen's Pride and Prejudice and Vyasa's Mahabharata.

From the other side, they explain the 'Physics of Wall Street' – quantitative models that have transformed twentieth century finance. I was particularly impressed by how they illustrate both the intuitive and counter intuitive dimensions of probability theory with examples that will surely make this book a useful compendium to any college text book on the subject. Similarly, they show how the celebrated theories and models of a stellar galaxy of scholars such Bachelier, Sharpe, Fama and Ross gave finance an intellectual heft and reshaped financial engineering.

At the heart of this book is the thesis that human behaviour influences financial markets in ways that we barely recognize. The way the book brings together the seemingly disparate expositions from hard and soft sciences to substantiate and explain that central thesis will rank as its defining feature. The storyline draws from historical experiences to show how the world goes from one financial crisis to another because people repeat the same follies as if they never learn anything from the past. History inevitably repeats itself, but contrary to the popular surmise, almost always as a tragedy.

If humans, with a head and a heart, are driven by emotions, can machines, with just a head, do any better? Will the combination of a fallible, irrational human and a cold, calculating machine prove to be optimal? Or will the conflict between the heart of the human and the mind of the machine end in a zero-sum game? These are tantalizing questions with answers all in the realm of speculation. Read this book to get a flavour of what the future might look like.

This book by the father-daughter duo is commendable on many counts – the clarity of its central message, the richness of concepts and ideas from a wide canvas, the engaging writing style with illustrations drawn from a variety of human experiences, its logical structure and the easy flow of the storyline. It's commendable most of all because Ramasastri and Aparajitha address a topic that is of vital importance.

This book will give you a better understanding of financial markets; more importantly, it will give you a better understanding of yourself.

My best wishes to Ramasastri and Aparajitha for the success of this book and for follow on books in the future taking off from where they finish here.

Duvvuri Subbarao
Governor (2008-13)
Reserve Bank of India

Preface

Motivation

We both have keen interest in probability theory, artificial intelligence, human behaviour and casinos, not necessarily in that order. Interestingly, we find the intersections of our areas of interest with stock markets. It is such common intersections that excited us to write the book *You, Games and Markets*.

The book is not a manual to make money in stock markets. It is a guide to help you to assess your ability to take rational decisions. According to us, such an ability is very much required in your life always and specifically during your buy and sell decisions in stock markets. You may wonder why anyone would take irrational decisions!

Each human is endowed not only with intelligence to think but also with emotions to feel. Though human brain is capable of taking decisions rationally, human emotions, at times, distort human rationality. Irrational behaviour can lead to errors in judgement and flaws in decisions, which are quite often risky and sometimes even ruinous.

In order to avoid such consequences from irrational decisions, it will be useful for you to understand your basic emotional traits. Self-understanding is the first step towards keeping away from hasty decisions driven by emotions and moving towards rational decisions backed by logic. The theme throughout our book is self-assessment for being better prepared to participate in stock markets. We organized the chapters of the book accordingly.

Organization

Chapter I deals with emotions, traits and personality of a human.

Chapter II identifies negative emotions that can distort rational decision making of a human.

Chapter III presents a series of simulated games which can help readers to assess their emotional traits. The traits are linked to market participant behavioural types. Understanding traits and types helps participants to avoid irrational decisions while buying and selling in stock markets.

Chapter IV is on Quantitative Methods required for stock markets. We discussed just the minimal concepts, which according to us are essential to stock market participants. We tried to make discussions intuitive, sacrificing mathematical rigour. Our intention is to give enough conceptual clarity to readers, especially to understand stock market theories discussed in Chapter V. Towards end of the chapter, we tried to tie knots between quantitative methods and their applications in stock markets.

Chapter V focusses on stock market theories. Some of the theories assume rational behaviour of market participants. The assumption is valid to a great extent at aggregate level as irrationalities are likely to be cancelled. But at an individual level, the irrationalities matter as they can prejudice investment decisions. The aim of our book is to assist retail investors in understanding their personality traits and market theories in order to take right buy and sell decisions. It is for this reason that we discussed important behavioural finance theories.

Chapter VI illustrates a few historical market events that went through bubbles and bursts. Human traits such as greed, herd mentality and fear were behind ecstasy and exodus of the events. The purpose of the chapter is to show the readers various phases of an asset bubble from excitement to exit. Knowing the past, we hope, can help in not repeating the same mistakes.

Chapter VII is on emotionless Artificial Intelligence (AI) Machines trading in the markets. We discuss various possibilities and consequences when human traders and AI based traders co-exist. Though emotions may be advantageous at times, they are, in general, detrimental to rational decision making. Machines may prove superior to humans in taking rational decisions, unaffected by greed, fear and even disappointments.

Chapter VIII is a summary of what was learnt in the book and how to use the learnings; our tips to the stock market participants.

Style

The topics in the book flow from human emotions that distort decisions to emotionless AI based trading in stock markets. We discussed other relevant topics like quantitative methods and market theories in between, taking adequate care to retain the flow of the book. Throughout the book, you travel with your emotions and their impact on your rational decision making ability. The idea is to alert you to take cognizance of your emotions, even if you are not able to get rid of them.

We tried to follow a direct style, as though talking to you. We constructed examples to elucidate the points we made. We used characters from classics to illustrate human traits. We provided self-tests to assist you to reflect on the ideas discussed. We supplemented with tables and figures, wherever we felt that they would add value. In addition, we presented a few points to ponder through self-assessment.

We tried our best not to use equations and formulas although we are aware that there is ease and convenience in mathematical symbols for explaining quantitative methods and market theories. Yet, we refrained from using them to keep the non-mathematically-oriented comfortable. There may be a few symbols in Chapters IV and V, which we could not avoid.

We included quotations at the beginning of each section, which we strongly feel, will add to your armour of knowledge and wisdom.

Acknowledgements

Let us first thank Dr Duvvuri Subbarao garu, who gracefully agreed to read our book and write

Foreword to it. His Foreword adds immense value to the book.

We thank innumerable number of researchers in the fields of behavioural finance and artificial intelligence for the insights we received from their articles and books. We thank the casinos we visited across the globe for the first-hand experience we gained on chance games and unguarded human behaviour. We thank our friends, and in particular Mr Jayakumar, a senior official from Reserve Bank of India, for taking time to meticulously go through the draft chapters and giving us feedback.

Finally, we thank Dr Gayatridevi, who as wife and mother, enthused us continuously to complete our book. And we also thank each other for encouraging, educating and empowering in our endeavour.

We trust you will benefit from the book.

AS Ramasastri
A Aparajitha

CHAPTER I

You Are What Your Emotions Are

Abstract

Emotions like fear, lust and greed have been playing an important role in ensuring survival and procreation of all living beings on this planet. As humans evolved over thousands of years, their requirements changed. But their basic emotions continue to dominate them. The emotions at times interfere with the rational and logical behaviour of humans.

Keywords

Emotions, Moods, Traits, Personality, Behaviour

1. Brain and Rational Behaviour

> *cogito, ergo sum*
> *I think, therefore I am*
> - René Descartes

Your brain is the most complex organ of your body. It is made up of billions of neurons that communicate in trillions of connections called synapses. Such an enormous neural network receives inputs, sorts, stores, analyses, builds indexes, links, and when required, retrieves. This description of human brain is purely from its function as a data processing engine, *a la* a computer. From this view point, brain is very rational and logical.

Fortunately and unfortunately, your brain, in addition to being the seat of intelligent processing, is also the seat of emotions, feelings and sentiments.

We say fortunately because it is your emotions that empower you to act decisively in difficult situations. But for your emotions, you would never think you would ever do some daring actions. We say unfortunately because as a bundle of emotions, it distracts you from an unbiased decision making process. To understand, let us consider some examples.

YOU, GAMES AND MARKETS 3

Example 1.1

Imagine you are in a village during a leisurely weekend. You suddenly see a hut on fire and a helpless old lady inside the burning hut. Under the normal circumstances, your rational brain does not allow you to run into a burning hut. However, a strong emotion of empathy overrides your logical thinking process. You rush into the hut without giving a thought to the sense of danger and save the old lady. When you recollect the event some time later, you may say "I did not think at that moment, I just dashed in to save that helpless lady"

It is the emotion of empathy that drives you to help. It is a moment of action and not reason. If only you got a little more time to think, it is difficult to say if you would have really run into the fire.

Example 1.2

Suppose you are enjoying a dinner with your friends on the roof-top restaurant of a thirty storey luxurious hotel adjacent to a sea. You suddenly hear a sound that resembled a gun shot in a floor just below roof top. Unconsciously your mind recalls an earlier occasion when you got stuck in a hotel in Mumbai, India as terrorists took seize of the hotel.

Panic strikes you and you immediately run down the stairs without thinking about the lovely dinner and safety of your friends.

Under the normal circumstances you may not run at all. Even if you did, you may never run fast. That too so awkwardly from the roof of a building. And most shamelessly leaving your friends in danger. But in fear, your behaviour is totally different.

Fear strays your brain away from its usual rational thoughts. You yourself would later recollect the event with remorse "I can't understand why I ran away like that – It was such a frightful moment that I lost all my logic"

Example 1.3

We have a personal experience to share with you - how our emotions pumped adrenaline in us to do what we would otherwise not do.

During the summer of 1998 we went on a vacation to Ooty, in Tamilnadu, India. We were then aged 40 and 10. Ooty is at a height of 2240 meters above sea level. A meter gauge train (joyfully called as a toy train) runs between the ground level Mettupalayam and hill top Ooty. Though the distance is only 46 kilometres, the train takes about 4-1/2 hours to go up and 3-1/2 hours to come down. It takes so long because of the steep ascent and descent. Further, it has to negotiate around 200 curves, pass through 16 tunnels and cross about 250 bridges / culverts *en route*.

After a happy 4-day stay in Ooty, we started our journey downhill by the train. The train started at 2 PM in Ooty and was scheduled to reach Mettupalayam by 5.30 PM. We were enjoying the breathtakingly beautiful scenic journey until the train stopped abruptly with a thud.

We came to know that the brakes failed and the train would not move. We also came to know that the railway authorities would not be able to arrange an alternative and that the only way for all the passengers was to walk to a point where they meet the road. We started walking down with two heavy suitcases and two bags. We did not know how long we had to walk to reach the road. There were guesses from other passengers, but none firm.

We had to walk only on track lest we should lose our way. After walking for a while on the track we realized that we had to cross bridges. The bridges that looked so beautiful when we crossed sitting in the train, looked treacherous when we walked on them. The valleys which appeared so attractive down below the bridge from the windows of the train, looked dangerous as we walked over them on the bridges.

We have acrophobia, fear for heights. We did not venture to any height any other time; especially if there was nothing to hold to; and worse if we had to see the deepness below us. On the railway tracks there was nothing to hold. Even if there was something there was no way to hold with suitcases and handbags in our hands. We had to walk knowing very well the danger of a fall, which is just fatal.

There was no way we could stop. We had to walk with weight of suitcases, fear of heights and onset of darkness. We had no time to think of any of these difficulties, leave alone rest, food or drink. The goal was to reach the road before day turns to night. And we did it, after walking for more than three hours, covering about ten kilometres, all because of the scary situation.

After more than two decades, we still ask ourselves – how could we do it? If we were asked to walk on the same track for three hours with similar weights, we would without any hesitation say NO.

But when we were faced with a do or die situation, we did the unthinkable. Survival instinct prevailed. Our fear of being left in woods in darkness gave us all necessary physical and mental strength. We survived the scary event to share it with you happily.

The examples amply illustrate that emotions can keep you pumped to do great things. But they can also distort your logical faculties and drive you to irrational decisions resulting in loss of wealth and also reputation. As our book is focussed on human behaviour in stock markets, we intend to devote the first three chapters to emotions, impact of negative emotions on human behaviour and understanding emotional traits with the help of simulated games.

Self-Assessment

Did you encounter any situation when you did an out of your normal behaviour to help yourself or someone else by sheer drive of an emotion?

Self-Assessment

Was there a situation when you left all your normal composure and demeanour due to an emotion and acted irrationally?

Don't hurry with answers. Reflect coolly. Write down the emotions and your actions.

NOTE : Be honest whenever you do Self-Assessment in this book. Remember that the self-assessments are to assist you and not to evaluate you!

2. Moods and Emotions

Our moods meet at wrong places
— Thomas Hardy

You might have used one of the following expressions some time or the other in your life.

"I am on cloud nine"
"I am shaken up"
"I am head over heels"
"I am on pins and needles"

The expressions reflect your moods of joy, shock, love and anxiety, respectively. In joy and love, you are in a good mood; in shock and anxiety in a bad mood.

When you are in a good mood, you tend to look at people and events around you with a positive disposition. However, when you are in a bad mood, you tend to see the world around you in a gloomy way, with a negative disposition towards people and events around you.

You might have experienced such moods on certain days, with or without any external reason. You are not alone in this world experiencing such moods;

many others experience some mood or the other at some time or the other.

The following three factors are considered to cause moods in us.

   a) Biology (hormones and brain chemicals)
   b) Psychology (innate and learned responses)
   c) Environment (illness and emotional stress)

Interestingly, the above three factors are considered to cause emotions as well. However, emotions are different from moods in the following three ways:

   a) Moods tend to be much more long-lasting, going for hours or days, whereas an emotion may only last for a few minutes or even seconds.
   b) Emotions are about something specific, such as a person or a situation, but moods are much more diffused with no identifiable object. A mood is a general feeling, not a reaction to a particular situation.
   c) Emotions can be strong feelings such as exhilaration, terror, or despair. Moods are not as intense as emotions. You might not be even consciously aware that you are in a good or bad mood until you notice them through your response to situations.

3. Emotions and Emotional Traits

*I don't want to be at the mercy of my emotions.
I want to use them, to enjoy them,
and to dominate them*

— Oscar Wilde

Let us consider a few examples to understand emotional traits.

Example 1.4

Your daughter walks into your room with a gold medal, she won in a national level quiz competition.

Seeing her achievement, your heart may race. Your face may flush. Your eyes may be filled with tears. These physical responses indicate that you are overwhelmed by the emotion of happiness. In addition to happiness, your daughter's achievement may also make you feel proud.

You hug her and tell her "I am proud"

Let us look at this statement closely. It can mean "I am proud of *you* for your success in quiz". It may also mean "I am in general a *proud* person"

The first sentence refers to your feeling of pride at that moment; it is an emotional feeling. The second sentence says that you are a proud person; it is your trait.

Example 1.5

Assume that a stranger came forward to help you when you landed in a difficult situation.

You feel a sense of gratefulness to the stranger and you tell her "I am grateful".

The sentence "I am grateful" can mean "I am grateful to *you* for your help" or "I am a *grateful* person"

While the first indicates your feeling of gratefulness to the stranger at that moment, the second characterizes you as a grateful person; it is your trait.

4. Emotional Traits and Personality

*Poetry is not a turning loose of emotion,
but an escape from emotion;
It is not the expression of personality
but an escape from personality.
But, of course, only those who have
personality and emotion
know what it means to want to escape from these*
— T.S. Eliot

Personality is unique to an individual. It is made up of a number of elements, which can be viewed as traits. Traits refer to various characteristics that assist in creating a personality.

While personality refers to the totality of characteristics which makes an individual unique, traits do not refer to the totality, but to the individual characteristics that contribute towards creating a personality.

For example, our personalities are made up of various traits such as kindness, aggression, greed, honesty, anger and envy.

But do such traits sustain in us? When we talk of sustainability we refer to two kinds of sustainability.

One is sustainability over situations. The other is sustainability over time.

Suppose you get angry in a particular situation, like when you see a dog physically abused. It is very likely that you become angry whenever you encounter a similar situation; not necessarily when a helpless animal like dog is abused; but also when a child or an elder is abused. It is your trait to get angry at such violence. The trait sustains in you and makes your personality.

Once a trait becomes part of your personality, you act quickly as per your trait even before you think.

Traits like anger, kindness, greed, envy, honesty and fear sustain in you over situations. These traits make your personality. Hence your personality sustains over situations.

The next question is about sustainability of traits or personality over time.

In general, the personality of a person gets formed around the age of 10-12 and crystallises by around the age of 18-20. Prior to the tweens, the traits exhibited by a child are more innate. They are temperamental in nature. They cannot be considered as personality traits, though they may become the building blocks for the personality development later.

Studies clearly indicate that traits, once crystallized sustain over time and stay with you for life. Many of the traits get entrenched in you and remain with you throughout your life. Your personality, which is a collection of you traits is likely to sustain over time, and make you what you are.

Self-Assessment

Is there any emotional trait in you, which is influencing your thoughts and actions in a similar way in similar situations? Write it down.

Self-Assessment

Is there any emotional trait in you that emerged after you turned 25? Is there any emotional trait in you that disappeared after you turned 25?

5. Traits – Positive and Negative

*No company is preferable to bad.
We are more apt to catch the vices
of others than virtues,
as disease is far more contagious than health*
— Charles Caleb Colton

Over centuries of civilization, traits have been characterized as virtues or vices. While some traits like humility are considered as virtues, traits like greed are considered as vices.

Religion played an important role in classifying traits as virtues and vices. The Table 1.1 indicates biblical view of virtues and vices. In general, the virtues are considered as positive traits and vices as negative traits.

Table 1.1 Biblical Virtues and Vices

Virtues	Vices (Deadly Sins)
Humility	Pride
Generosity	Greed
Chastity	Lust
Patience	Anger
Temperance	Gluttony
Charity	Envy
Diligence	Laziness

Other ancient religions like Hinduism, Taoism, and Buddhism also recognize certain traits as positive and certain others as negative.

There is no reason to disagree with such a classification of positive and negative traits by religions. We know very well that the religious leaders have done such a categorization keeping in view the overall good of every individual and the wellbeing of the society.

In this book, we will discuss only the negative traits. We have the following reasons for it:

- Though both positive and negative traits can distort your decision making ability, positive traits distort positively; they help you act in the overall interest of the society and not with your self-interest as objective. On the other hand, the negative traits are aimed at your self-interest; they destroy your logical and rational thinking process; leading to decisions that are likely to doom you.
- Negative traits lead to irrational behaviour of humans. The irrationality influences buy and sell decisions in stock markets. As our book is centred around the behavioural

aspects of market participants, our focus is on the negative traits.

We will discuss in detail in Chapter II about the consequences of negative traits on the people who possess them as well as on people around them.

6. Negative Traits that Matter

> *The greatest temptations are not those that solicit our consent to obvious sin, but those that offer us great evils masking as the greatest goods*
> — Thomas Merton

For the purpose of identifying the negative traits that impact us the most, let us take recourse to Indian theology. The theology recognizes six traits as enemy traits, which are together called as *arishadvarga* (group of six enemies). The six traits are:

- *kama* (lust)
- *krodha* (anger)
- *lobha* (greed)
- *moha* (attachment)
- *mada* (pride)
- *matsarya* (envy)

Though Indian theology has correctly identified the six traits as enemies to humans, we are excluding the trait *kama* as we don't find it very much relevant to behaviour of stock market participants, which is the focus of our book. According to us, even if *kama* (lust) is not included, *moha* (attachment) takes care of its negativities in the context of stock markets.

Instead of *kama* (lust) we are including *bhaya* (fear) in its place. We strongly feel that fear can distort your understanding of reality completely and quite often lead you to irrational behaviour and wrong decisions.

Thus, we will be discussing the following six traits in detail in Chapter II -

- Anger
- Greed
- Attachment
- Pride
- Envy
- Fear

7. Can you Escape your Emotions?

The best and most beautiful things in the world cannot be seen or even touched. They must be felt with the heart
— Helen Keller

Before we find out whether we can free ourselves from our emotions by constant and conscious effort, let us first understand the possible reasons why humans have emotions.

Let us agree that we do not know the real purpose of our existence on earth, a small planet amidst the vast universe of stars and galaxies. We can also agree that life has been on this planet for millions of years. It has been in existence despite several adverse situations.

It has been possible for life to continue because all living beings have been equipped with two natural instincts. First is Survival. Second is Procreation.

Why this grand design of universe desires life to continue to exist is a question, for which a definite answer is difficult to know. Despite advances in science and technology, explaining the macro and micro cosmos, humans may never know the answer.

As Stephen Hawking puts it - we may know how of the universe but never why of the universe.

However, in order to ensure continuity of life on this planet, all living beings, including humans have been endowed with necessary instincts and skills; and also with emotions like fear, anger, lust and attachment. Each emotion has its purpose. Fear helps to fight or flight from predators for survival. Lust is instrumental for procreation.

Through millions of years, the purpose of all living beings, other than humans has remained the same – survival and procreation. However, humans, over the past thousands of years, in the process of evolution, have developed intellectual abilities, including languages that made their lives more comfortable, yet complicated.

The complexities created in the process of development, are forcing humans to live with the same old innate natural emotions in the completely changed circumstances. Managing the primitive emotions, which they were endowed for survival and procreation, has become an immense challenge in the new world humans created around them.

Fear as an emotion is still dominant in humans, though they had moved out of the danger zone of predators quite some time back. As threat from strong animals to humans has gradually decreased, the emotion could have slowly disappeared. But it has not. Instead it is showing up its ugly face in other unwanted and unwarranted situations. For some it is fear of insects. For others it is fear of water. For some it is fear of facing public. For others it is loneliness. For some it is darkness. And for others it is unknown. Finally humans are affected by fear of fear!

As civilizations progressed, humans have also developed some nice thoughts like romance and platonic love. How primitive human emotion of lust gets manifested in an idealistic romantic world is not clear. It is possible that supressed lust may manifest to other emotions like aggression, anger, attachment and avarice.

Same is the case with other emotions. They surface in an unrecognized form and that too when they are not required. Humans themselves may not know why an unwanted emotion is affecting them and hindering their thought process. The challenge is becoming greater, as the pace of developments in science and technology is becoming quicker and its impact on humans is becoming stronger.

We are forced to adjust emotionally to a new world very quickly. Not all of us can make such an adjustment. Maladjustment is leading to mental health related problems, some serious; some not so serious but nevertheless impacting our behaviour.

Emotions are hard-wired into our body, wherever that wiring is – the brain or the nervous system, or the endocrine system; and for whatever reason the hard-wiring is – hereditary, habitat or habit.

We cannot escape from our emotions because emotions are responses to external stimuli for survival and procreation. Neither should we try to escape from them. We have to live with them. For that, we have to understand them and their nature. The chapter is an attempt to present the background for our emotions and our behaviour; it is, in a way, a primer to the remaining chapters of the book.

We end the chapter with a caveat – that we have not covered some topics related to emotional and personality traits in our book. We give the list of topics not covered by us. The interested reader to study standard books for a better grasp of the topics. As far as our book is concerned, we don't feel the need for a detailed discussion of the topics.

8. Caveat

The scope of this book is limited to understanding your emotions, impact of your emotions on your behaviour and impact of your behaviour on your decision making in stock markets. In order to not lose focus on the scope of the book, we are not discussing the following topics in this book:

a) The parts of brain like cerebrum, cerebellum and medulla
b) Neuron components like axons, dendrites and synapses
c) Action of chemicals like dopamine and serotonin on moods
d) Influence of glands and hormones on emotions
e) Evolution of human beings and their emotions
f) Role of language in evolution of human thoughts
g) Moods and mood disorders
h) Role of genetics and environment on personality
i) Nature and nurture of emotions
j) Religions, Morals, Ethics, Emotions and Control of Emotions

CHAPTER II

Negative Traits

Abstract

Emotional traits hinder with logical thought process and lead to irrational behaviour of humans. Especially the traits like pride, envy, anger, attachment, greed and fear have been proving negative to humans in their decision taking. Such traits have been the causes behind hasty buy and sell decisions in stock markets.

Keywords

Emotions, Emotional Traits, Anger, Greed, Fear, Attachment, Envy, Pride

1. Anger

Anybody can become angry — that is easy,
but to be angry with the right person
and to the right degree
and at the right time and for the right
purpose, and in the right way —
that is not within everybody's power and is not easy
— Aristotle

Getting angry is a normal human emotion. In fact, it sometimes helps you to be angry, especially when you have to be. You can't obviously remain unaffected when someone intentionally harms you. You may have to become angry when gross injustice is done to you and your survival is at stake.

Imagine, someone is rebuking you, or insulting or even physically attacking you. Your reaction needs to be an angry one. Anger, during such circumstances is a useful response. It is not negative.

But there are occasions when you get angry, you yourself realize later that it is not justified. It is possible that a friend pulls your leg as a prank. It is likely your spouse does not respond to your comment as per your expectation. Neither your friend nor your spouse has been intending to insult you. Yet you get angry. In the fit of anger you may shout at them.

Such unjustifiable anger is a negative emotion. Once you are free from anger you realize that your reaction was irrational and you regret your action. Anger becomes instrumental in hasty decisions and haughty reactions.

Let us learn about anger and its harms through two stories of *Panchatantra*. *Panchatantra* is an ancient Indian book of animal fables in *Sanskrit*, told within the frame of five main stories. The authorship of the work is attributed to *Vishnusarma*. Emotional traits are presented in the fables through animal characters, including the dangerous consequences of such traits.

Example 2.1

A man has two animals, a dog and a donkey - the donkey to carry loads and the dog to protect the house from thieves. One night when a thief enters the house, the dog does not bark. Sensing the danger, the donkey starts braying. The man wakes up and gets irritated with the braying of the donkey. Without thinking why the donkey is braying he beats the donkey to death. His anger does not allow him to reflect for a moment why the donkey has been braying. In the process he not only loses his valuables to the thieves, but also his donkey to his anger. All because his anger does not allow him to think rationally.

Example 2.2

A family rears a mongoose as pet. When parents go out for work, the mongoose takes care of the house and the child. One day a snake sneaks into the house and goes towards the child. Seeing the danger, the mongoose jumps on the snake and kills it. The child is saved. However, when the mother enters the house and sees pieces of flesh and blood, she suspects that mongoose killed her child. Enraged, she kills the mongoose with a stick. Her anger does not allow her to think before she acts.

The two examples highlight how irrational humans become due to anger!

It is difficult to be free from anger altogether. However, what is important to know is whether anger is your dominant trait or not. To know whether anger dominates you or not ask yourself three questions – how often you get angry, how intense your anger is and how long does it last. The following self-tests help you to make an assessment of your anger.

Self-Test 2.1 (Frequency)

In the apartment complex where you are residing, a few children play football in the corridor of your floor every evening from 6 PM to 7 PM. As you return from your office around 6.30 PM, you invariably pass through the corridor to reach your apartment. In their total involvement in the game, the children ignore you and continue to play as you pass by them. Do you get angry -

  a) every day
  b) on the days you are otherwise in bad mood
  c) on days when boys look more callous
  d) you won't get angry at all

Self-Test 2.2 (Intensity)

In your office, an opportunity for promotion arises for which, you and one of your colleagues are eligible. There is a general feeling among your peers that you deserve it. But the management has decided to promote your colleague instead of you. Do you -

  a) resign your job, in a fit of anger

b) immediately apply for a long leave
c) shout at your friends and family members
d) go to the office as usual

Self-Test 2.3 (Recovery)

You just commenced a long drive, on a family holiday, to a distant mountain valley. As you are about to turn onto the highway, a motorist unexpectedly speeds past you, without bothering about road signs, signals and speed.

a) You laugh away at his childish behaviour
b) You pass on the information to the highway police and carry on
c) You first shout at your kids; quickly realize your folly and join them in the fun
d) You keep cribbing throughout the drive, spoiling the fun

We can call the above three self-tests together as FIR tests – Frequency-Intensity-Recovery tests. FIR test can be used not only to assess anger but also other emotional traits.

Remember that there are no standard scores for these self-tests. There are two ways to use the tests. One is by repeating the tests over a period of time; to check if you have improved over time. Second is to see how you fare in comparison with your friends and family.

Let us reiterate that you should be honest in self-tests and self-assessments.

2. Greed

Earth provides enough to satisfy every man's needs, but not every man's greed
— Mahatma Gandhi

We can describe greed as desire which is more than what is decent or deserved; solely for selfish interest; possibly detrimental to society at large.

Greed is a primitive trait, ingrained into our genes for our survival and procreation. However, unlike other living beings, humans exhibit greater degree of greed as they look at their needs for a longer span of time, till their death and even beyond it.

Also, the objects of human greed are not just food and sex for survival and reproduction. They have moved far beyond - to money, worldly possessions, power and fame. Further, the desire is not just confined to objects of desire, but to desire itself!

Greed is a primitive trait and is generally useful if it is within limits. But when it crosses all reasonableness then it is a dangerous negative trait. It is so negative that it can push the greedy person down the abyss to any depth.

As illustrations of greedy characters, let us look closely at *Pakhom* from the short story, *How much Land Does a Man Need?* written by *Leo Tolstoy* and *Macbeth* from the play *Macbeth* written by *William Shakespeare*.

Example 2.3

Pakhom, a Russian peasant, has been working very hard for his survival. Unexpectedly he gets an opportunity to own as much land as he can walk in a day. The only condition is that he has to come back to the starting point before the sun sets. Fuelled by his excessive desire for more land, he ignores his draining energies and keeps walking. Even when he is finding it difficult to move, he still says to himself, "An hour to suffer, a life-time to live." By the sunset, he is totally exhausted. Finally, when he reaches the place where he started, he dies of the strain. Eventually, he needed only six feet of land from his head to his heels for his burial.

Example 2.4

In the famous tragedy of Shakespeare, *Macbeth*, the hero ends up as epitome of greed. In the beginning of the play, *Macbeth* is a very humble man. It is the prophecy of the three witches that sows in him the seed of desire to become the king. Added to his desire is the guidance from his ambitious wife, *Lady Macbeth*. The desire grows into greed unabated and he kills *King Duncan*. Thereafter he arranges to kill *Banquo* and *Macduff*'s family. Throughout the story, Macbeth lets his desire to turn into greed. And through the character of Macbeth, Shakespeare shows what all greed can do.

Self-Test 2.4

You get a phone call on your mobile. A sweet, smooth, soothing voice checks whether you are alone or with someone else. Once you confirm you that are alone, the voice says that a rich man in Austria died intestate. However, you can claim his riches provided you sign a few documents making first claim of the wealth. The voice assures you that it is a genuine and lawful transaction. However, the news should not be leaked as that would create a social media ruckus. The voice asks you to share your email id and address to forward the documents and requests you to do all the activities very quickly and in secrecy. At your end all that is required is to pay a small processing fee, which is miniscule compared to what you would inherit. What will you do?

a) Pay at once the processing fee in secrecy

YOU, GAMES AND MARKETS 37

b) Wait for a day, get a few more doubts clarified and then pay
c) Ignore the offer, but keep repenting you lost a golden opportunity
d) Forget the whole phone call as a hoax and enjoy the fun

Self-Test 2.5

You are a mother of twelve year old child. The child is preparing for a scholarship test at her school. A day before the test, your daughter receives hints on the likely questions. Your daughter is about to pick up her mobile phone and talk to her friends to share the information she received. You know very well that the school would select only three students for the scholarship.

What do you do?

a) You encourage your daughter to share the information with all her friends.
b) You dissuade your daughter from sharing the information with bright students.
c) You order her sternly not to share the information with anyone else.
d) You allow her to share information only with two of her best friends

3. Attachment

You only lose what you cling to
— Gautama Buddha

The *Bhagavadgita*, in short the *Gita*, was told by *Krishna*, the philosopher-statesman of ancient India, to *Arjuna*, a brave warrior of the *Mahabharata*. What an irony it is, that the brave warrior loses his composure to fight the most important battle of his life. *Arjuna* sees all his relatives in the enemy camp and loses interest in the battle as he has to kill them. When he pleads with *Krishna* to let him leave the battle field, *Krishna* counsels him. While counselling, *Krishna* describes the perils of attachment. He says -

While contemplating the objects of the senses,
a person develops attachment for them;
from such attachment lust develops;
from lust anger and from anger delusion arise;
delusion leads to bewilderment of memory;
When memory is bewildered, intelligence is lost.

Krishna describes logically the process of downfall from attachment through lust, anger, delusion, and bewilderment to the loss of your rational thinking.

Quite often, people confuse between love and attachment. Love is a form of generosity. It is a state of mind in which you feel an inner peace. Attachment, on the other hand, is a state of mind characterized by clinginess, greed, and possessiveness.

In love, you feel secure, even when your loved one is not physically with you. There is stability and understanding about your loved one's affection, care, and feelings whereas attachment is characterized by insecurity, suspicion and dependence.

The *Mahabharata*, an epic of ancient India in hundred thousand verses composed by *Veda Vyasa*, is a treasure of both worldly wisdom and otherworldly spiritualism. The epic has several complex characters and curious circumstances that explain personality traits, behavioural peculiarities and their consequences. Let us understand the trait of attachment through *Dhritarashtra*, an important character in the epic.

Example 2.5

As *Dhritarashtra* was born blind, he was denied the throne of *Hastinapura*. Though anointed as the king, his younger brother, *Pandu*, preferred to stay away from the kingdom. *Dhritarashtra* was so attached to the throne and crown that he agreed to be the king, despite his blindness.

Duryodhana, his son, was younger than *Yudhishtara*, the son of Pandu. There was a tussle for crown between the two cousins – both having their reasons for the claim. *Dhritarashtra* is very much attached to his son. Due to excessive attachment, he remained a silent spectator to the misdeeds of his son, which included attacking his cousins, cheating them in gamble, denying them the kingdom and disrobing their queen. He did not heed to the advice of wise men of his court who forewarned him about the ensuing Mahabharata battle and the loss of several lives.

He was born blind not only in his eyes; but also in his mind. His mind was blinded by excessive attachment to the throne and son. He was greatly responsible for the *Mahabharata* war, in which his family died. What an abyss his attachment threw him and his family into!

Example 2.6

Two women go to a judge, each claiming a baby boy as her child and requesting for the custody of the child. After several rounds of queries and enquiries, the judge is not able to find the real mother. In order to satisfy both the women, the judge suggests cutting the child into two halves and hand over a half to each woman. One of the women, immediately declines the suggestion. She says that as a mother, she cannot allow the child to die. She is fine losing the custody of the child, but not losing the child. The judge orders custody of the child to the woman and imprisonment of the other, saying that the real mother truly loves the child.

Self-Test 2.6

You are at an airport to see your spouse off, who is going on a business trip to Mauritius for two weeks. Your marriage anniversary is just a week away. You are not able to go because of your commitments. You are aware that your spouse would be taken care by a childhood friend in Mauritius. You are also aware that the friend is very affectionate to your spouse. Do you feel -

a) Insecure
b) Suspicious
c) Indifferent
d) Happy that your spouse is getting quality time with a close friend

Self-Test 2.7

On a bright sunny day, you get an idea that you will be able to reduce your weight by half if you follow a diet and exercise regime. Your spouse does not approve of the plan as it is not backed by any medical research. Your children too do not support your idea. Your friends advise you not to follow the diet as they know some people who suffered due to a similar diet-exercise regime. However, you do not want to leave your idea. Not because you have any evidence that it works, but because it is *your* idea. Choose the right option among the following:

 a) You love your idea
 b) You are attached to your idea

4. Pride

Vanity and pride are different things, though the words are often used synonymously. A person may be proud without being vain. Pride relates more to our opinion of ourselves, vanity to what we would have others think of us
— Jane Austen

Pride is both a virtue and a vice. It is a virtue to the extent of you loving your own excellence. It is recognizing your worth yourself. It is proper pride.

However, if it is an inflated sense of your worth, it is no more a virtue. It is an empty claim of your worth only in your own imagination. It is a vanity. Such a pride is a vice.

Pride rears its head even in the most unsuspected corners. While some may be proud that they are proud, some others may be proud that they are not proud. While one may be proud of being a non-believer, another may be proud of being devoted to God. Learning may render one proud, and yet ignorance can be the source of pride for another.

You keep hearing the words ego, arrogance and vanity along with pride. They are in no way synonyms. By understanding each of the words, you may get a better understanding of pride.

According to Sigmund Freud's psychoanalytic theory, there are three parts to the personality - the id, the ego, and the superego. The ego is the psychological component of your personality that is represented by your conscious decision-making process. However, in the common parlance, an inflated ego is associated with narcissistic tendencies, superiority complex, and being self-absorbed.

Arrogance is a sense of one's own greatness. It is the feeling of one's superiority over others. Arrogance is too self-satisfied to see any good in others. An arrogant person is unwarrantably overbearing and haughty; not only thinks highly of self but poorly of others; claims much for self and concedes little to others.

Vanity craves admiration and applause. It is an undue over assumption of self-importance. It often results in open and rude expression of contempt and hostility. It quickly takes for granted superiority and privilege, even when others recognize it as vanity.

We present various states of your pride based on your worthiness and your perception of your worthiness in the Table 2.1.

Table 2.1 Various States of Pride

YOU	think you are worthy	think you are not worthy
are worthy	Proper Pride	Pusillanimous
are not worthy	Vanity	Temperate

Jane Austen excelled in portraying pride through her characters in the novel, *Pride and Prejudice*. Let us look at two characters, *Lady Catherine* and *Darcy* in the following two examples.

Example 2.7

Lady Catherine is proud because she was born an aristocrat, raised to believe herself to be superior to others. She is patronizing, believes she has a right to know and judge everything and gives petty advices because she needs to feel useful. She always likes to be the centre of attention, and she expects to always be obeyed. Her pride is caricatured to be obnoxious by *Austen*.

Example 2.8

The chief representative of pride in the novel is *Darcy*. The introduction of his character reveals his pride. He seems withdrawn, superior and cynical. He puts *Elizabeth* down coldly with a patronising comment about her looks. Later, despite his infatuation, he feels himself superior to *Elizabeth*. Even his proposal to *Elizabeth* reflects less of tenderness and more of pride; as though he is doing her a favour. She is outraged and accuses him of arrogance and conceit.

Self-Test 2.8

Prepare a table giving the qualities you consider as your worth. Show it to ten friends. Based on your list, let them indicate your trait as one of the following:

   a) Proper Pride
   b) Pusillanimous
   c) Vanity
   d) Temperate

Compile the responses of your friends. Compare your view of your trait with the views of majority.

Self-Test 2.9

Pride has a tendency to manifest itself into other negative traits. Can you pick from the list below, the traits pride can manifest into?

   a) Envy
   b) Anger
   c) Revenge
   d) All three

5. Envy

*Our envy always lasts longer than
the happiness of those we envy*
— François Duc de La Rochefoucauld

The statements below signify the deadly nature of the trait, Envy.

"Envy is the most shameful of deadly sins"

"Envy blinds you to the bigger picture"

"Envy costs you friends, allies and relationships"

"Envy leads to more Envy"

To understand the trait better, let us try to differentiate between envy and its closely associated trait, jealousy. While jealousy relates to possessive nature, signifying fear of losing possessions to others, envy relates to covetousness, signifying desire for possessions of others. The scale moves from jealous to possessive to covetous to envious – from fear of losing to longing to possess.

Envy may even lead to feeling pleasure at misfortune of others and at the news of fallen celebrities. In fact it is this characteristic of envy that makes it more difficult to admit, compared to jealousy. There is shame in admitting your envy not only to others but also to yourself.

The objects of your envy can range from tangibles like money and land to invisibles like beauty, intelligence, popularity and fame.

Let us pick characters from two great epics, from *India* and *Greece* – the *Mahabharata* written by *Veda Vyasa* and the *Iliad* written by *Homer*. Both the authors had accomplished an incredible mission of putting together several characters of varying shades, their interactions, and consequences of their behavioural traits.

Example 2.9

In the Mahabharata, *Duryodhana* is the personification of envy. His envious personality has been visible from his early days, when he goes to the extent of attempting to kill his cousins. As they survive his attempts, his envy breeds more envy. It goes to such an extent that he tricks them to lose a gamble. He banishes them from the kingdom for thirteen long years. After completing the term of banishment, when they seek their kingdom back he declines. Even when they are prepared to accept five small hamlets instead of their share of kingdom, he does not yield. His envy blinds him. He paves way for a great war, in which he, his brothers, relatives and friends die.

Example 2.10

In the *Iliad*, *Hera* is the queen of the gods. She is the goddess of women, marriage, family and childbirth. She is one of the twelve *Olympians*. She is the sister and wife of *Zeus*. Her husband has relationships with other women, which drives her to envy.

Paris, the Prince of *Troy*, once says that the goddess *Aphrodite* is prettier than *Hera*. She grows envious of *Aphrodite* and angry of *Paris*. Hence, during the *Trojan* war between the *Greeks* and the *Trojans*, she always takes the side of the *Greeks* - although as a goddess she is not supposed to support either.

Self-Test 2.10

You belong to the lower middle income group. Your work in a relatively obscure department of a multinational company. Who is likely to be first target of your envy?

   a) Billionaire owner of your company

b) Head of your department, whom you may meet once in a year
c) Your co-employee who is tipped to get two months' salary as bonus
d) The waiter in your office restaurant, who receives tips half of your salary

Self-Test 2.11

You post your photo wearing a new dress on social media. Immediately, you start counting likes and reading comments. You go to bed, feeling very happy with the number of likes and comments. You wake up next morning and look through the social media. The responses to your photo have not increased. You feel disappointed.

Suddenly, you see another photo posted a couple of hours after you posted your photo. The number of likes is at least ten times that of yours. Comments on the photo are flattering, to say the least. One of the comments says, "even at this age you look more gorgeous than your daughter". That daughter is you. What is your emotion at that point of time?

a) Happy to have such a beautiful mother

b) Amused at the comments
c) Relook at your photo and wonder what is really wrong
d) Envious of your mother

6. Fear

*Don't give in to your fears. If you do,
you won't be able to talk to your heart*
— Paulo Coelho

A few synonyms for fear are apprehension, fright, dread, terror, trepidation, horror and timidity. Some antonyms are assurance, confidence, courage, fearlessness, trust and boldness. We would like to add hope as an important antonym for fear. If hope is one side of the coin, fear is the other side.

Fear is a natural primitive trait in living beings. It helps in protecting them from attacks of predators. In fear, the prey can choose to fight or flight.

Extreme fear drives you to extreme misery. Life becomes so terrible that you tend to miss several opportunities, due to fear – fear of imperfection, fear of loss, fear of defeat, fear of public criticism and fear of unknown.

Plato puts it succinctly –

*We can easily forgive a child who
is afraid of the dark;
the real tragedy of life is when
men are afraid of the light*

Example 2.11

In the *Hindu* mythology, there is a character named *Kamsa*. Immediately after he gets his sister, *Devaki*, married, he hears an oracle voice warning him that the eighth son born to *Devaki* would kill *Kamsa*. *Kamsa* is a strong man and great warrior. However, fear grips him on hearing the warning.

Despite his love for his sister, he imprisons her and her newly married husband. As *Devaki* delivers her first son, *Kamsa* kills him. Though the warning is only about eighth son, his fear does not allow him to be peaceful with any son of *Devaki*. He keeps killing *Devaki*'s sons as they are born.

As per mythology, the God, *Krishna* himself is born to *Devaki* as her eighth child. Through a miracle, *Krishna* transports himself to a faraway village. Not finding the eighth boy, *Kamsa* becomes restless. He sends his solders to locate the missing boy and kill. The hunt goes on for more than eight years. And during all these eight years, *Kamsa* leads a miserable life in utter fear. At the end of eight long years, *Kamsa* gets killed by *Krishna*. But *Kamsa* must have died every moment of his life till his actual death, as indicated in the maxim - "the brave dies only once, the coward dies every moment"

Example 2.12

In *the Harry Potter* series, *Hermione* is a very likeable character that will be remembered for ages. Whether it is her intelligence, love for knowledge, or wit, Hermione Granger is like no other. *In the Prisoner of Azkaban, Hermione's Boggart* takes the form of Professor *McGonagall* telling *Hermione* that she has failed all of her exams. *Hermione's* biggest fear is fear of failure. Even an intelligent and successful girl like *Hermione* has fear of failure!

Self-Test 2.12

You are invited to give a talk at a reputed institution in another city. As your talk is at 10 AM, you plan to go the previous night to the institution and spend the night at their hostel. Your host suggested you stay at a nearby hotel, but you felt it would be better to stay inside the campus.

You plan your flight in such a way that you reach the hostel on time for dinner. Unfortunately, the flight gets delayed. The institution driver picks you and drives you to the institution. Once you reach the institution at almost midnight, the main gate security hands over the room key. The hostel is in a corner of the institution, surrounded by trees. It is an old building, which is poorly lit. You try to ignore the negatives and go to bed without dinner. You sense eeriness all around.

Suddenly, the phone in your room rings. You pick up and hear your host voice "I got a message from our security that you checked into the hostel. I understand your flight is delayed. I hope the hostel is comfortable to you. Some guests do not like to stay there as they feel it is a haunted house with ghosts all around you during night. But you are brave. You did not go to a hotel, though I was hinting the alternative. Please have a pleasant night". As the conversation ended, what do you feel –

- a) Anger at the host for disturbing you at night
- b) Amusement at his words about ghosts in the hostel
- c) Scared of the situation, but sure you would be safe as you don't believe ghosts
- d) Unable to bear the fear, spend a sleepless night

Self-Test 2.13

You are working in a big tech company and your team won a major software development project with a large aircraft company. You are the key person in your team, who knows all the intricacies of the project. When a demonstration of the software was arranged to the president of the aircraft company, in the presence of the president of your company, you were assigned the responsibility of the demonstration. You have never done public speaking anytime in your life. One or two attempts during your school days ended up in a fiasco. You have not yet overcome the fear of public speaking.

For somebody of your age and position, it is a golden opportunity. If your demonstration goes well, there are bright chances of a pay raise and promotion.

What do you do?

   a) Decline the assignment, citing your stage fear as the reason.
   b) Accept, but pretend to be ill just a day before demonstration
   c) Do the presentation, but a bit badly, because of your lack of confidence
   d) Take help of team members, prepare well, and do a very good presentation

We did not originally include two traits – pessimism and quixotism in the list of negative traits. However, taking into account their potential to affect your behaviour in stock markets, we are presenting a few self-tests for your understanding and assessment.

7. Pessimism

We are all in the gutter, but some of us are looking at the stars
— Oscar Wilde

Self-Test 2.14

From your early teens, you have been seeing your mother suffering in the hands of your father. Your mother keeps cursing herself for getting attracted to his physical features and ignoring to assess his emotional traits like arrogance and envy. Despite hardships in his hands, your mother has not divorced your father for the sake of your happiness.

Once you are in early twenties, a handsome man proposes to you. When you discuss the proposal with your mother, she strongly recommends to accept. She supports him due to his brilliant academic and professional achievements, in addition to his attractive looks.

Will you -

a) Reject because you believe that marriage is not good for women
b) Reject because you lost trust in men in general

c) Reject because you feel that attractive men have bad emotional traits
d) Accept leaving behind the bad experience of your mother

Self-Test 2.15

You, along with a few friends, plan a trip to *Manasa Sarovar* in the India-China border through a tour operator. A week prior to your departure, another group travelling through the same tour operator, gets stranded half-way due to heavy snowfall. You discuss with your friends about your plan in view of the recent incidents. You propose cancellation. Your friends feel that you are pessimistic. Under the circumstances, do you feel you are -

a) Pessimistic
b) Superstitious
c) Overcautious
d) Realistic

8. Quixotism

In order to attain the impossible,
one must attempt the absurd
- Miguel de Cervantes

Self-Test 2.16

In your school days, while learning about great discoveries and inventions, you and some of your friends used to think that you would come out with a world shattering study someday. Possibly converting copper into gold. Or a machine with perpetual motion. Or a gene that gives immortality to a human. As you grow, you start feeling that such things are fantasy. You start working only on feasible and realizable projects.

However, a friend of yours still holds one such fantastic idea in her mind, even after she turns fifty. Working at a reputed global university, she believes that she will achieve her goal one day. What do you and your friends assess her to be?

    a) Unrealistic
    b) Romantic
    c) Dreamy
    d) Tenacious

Self-Test 2.17

How will you rate yourself if you were the person in Self-Test 2.16? What chances do you give to yourself for achieving your goal?

Self-Test 2.18

You walk into a race course, with the experience of ninety nine visits behind you. During the previous visits, you observe that a white horse with black spots invariably wins. In your hundredth visit, you do not find such a horse. In the absence of the certain winner, you return without betting. What do you think your decision is based on?

- a) Knowledge
- b) Experience
- c) Superstition
- d) Quixotism

Self-Test 2.19

List down factors based on which you assess whether a person is pursuing a realistic goal or an unrealistic dream?

Self-Assessment

Based on examples and self-tests assess your dominant negative trait, by marking X in the box against the trait in the Table 2.2. It is possible that you have more than one dominant trait, in which case, mark X in each of the relevant boxes.

Table 2.2 Self-Assessment Table

Sl No	Enemy Trait	Put X mark
1	Anger	
2	Greed	
3	Attachment	
4	Pride	
5	Envy	
6	Fear	
7	Pessimism	
8	Quixotism	

CHAPTER III

Simulated Games

Abstract

There are pure skill games like chess, semi-skill games like bridge and chance games like roulette. Stock markets can never be pure skill games. They are at best semi-skill games but more often resemble chance games. Emotions play a major role in games. Simulated games help in self-assessment of emotional traits and personality. Self-assessment can help market participants to be better prepared.

Keywords

Casino, Games, Gamble, Motivation, Mind-Set, Risk Appetite, Aggressive, Conservative, Follower, Adventurist, Biased, Analytical, Trader, Investor, Speculator

1. Are Stock Markets Casinos?

> *Not only does God play dice,*
> *but he sometimes throws them*
> *where they cannot be seen*
> - Stephen Hawking

There are games like chess and billiards, where you will win if you are better skilled than your opponent. They are pure skill games.

Games like rummy and bridge are semi-skill. When cards are dealt, it is possible that cards in one hand are better than the other. Thereafter, skill is required to play in the best possible way with the given distribution of cards. They are strategy games.

In the case of games like ludo and monopoly, it is mainly chance that matters, though an element of strategy helps. They are chance games.

When it comes to games in casino, there is hardly any skill or strategy. They are chance games.

Self-Test 3.1

Where do you place stock markets in terms of skill and chance?

a) 100% Skill
b) 50% Skill
c) 10% Skill
d) 1% Skill

Motivations and Mind-Sets

To understand the skill set levels of stock market participants, let us first look at their motivation. It is to make profit. Very few, if at all there are, may participate in the market without a profit motive.

Though making profit is the common motivation, there are basically three mind-sets behind the motivation. They are speculation, investment and trading.

As far as a speculator is concerned, the objective is to make high profits irrespective of the risk associated with it. In the case of traders and investors, the objective is to make reasonable profits at an acceptable level of risk.

From the risk perspective, speculation is very close to gambling. Investing is relatively less of gambling compared to trading. Let us do a pairwise comparison of speculation, investment and trading.

Speculation and Investment

a) Buying a stock with the anticipation that its price would increase is speculation. The aim of it is not investment. The approach is not necessarily analytical. The speculator is willing to take any risk. On the other hand, investing involves thorough analysis of the company and belief in its long-term growth potential. The investor chooses to invest after ascertaining that the probability of a large loss is low.

b) A speculator holds the stock for a short time or a long time depending on the price movements. But an investor, unlike the speculator, plans to hold the stock for a long time.

c) The difference between the attitudes of speculator and investor become prominent when the stock price starts falling. A speculator will get rid of the loser at a predetermined point.

An investor analyzes why the price is dropping and will determine whether it is a short-term situation or a change that will have a long-term impact on the stock's price.

Trading and Speculation

Traders are not interested in long term investment. They try to manage profits by buying low and selling high during short spans. Apparently, trading may look like speculation. But there are differences.

a) Trading is disciplined, speculation is not.
b) Trading estimates the outcome, speculating guesses the outcome
c) Trading is about managing risk, speculating is about betting on risk

Trading and Investment

Trading and investment differ from speculation; but they also differ between each other.

a) The main difference between investing and trading is the time horizon they are looking at. The trader goes for a short-term investment, say a few months, weeks, or days. Intraday traders, in fact, buy and sell shares within a single trading day. An investor, however, leans towards long-term investment, for at least a year or sometimes up to 3-5 years.

b) The second difference is their risk appetite. Risk appetite of trader is in general higher than investor.

c) The psychologies of a trader and an investor differ. Traders keep watching price cycles closely, think on their feet and take decisions quickly. Investors are patient and take their time for decision making.

Based on the discussions so far, we present skill and risk of speculator, trader and investor in the Table 3.1

Table 3.1 Skill and Risk of various Mind-Sets

Mind-Set	Skill	Risk
Speculator	Low	High
Trader	Medium / High	Medium
Investor	High	Low

In Sum,

- If the majority of stock market participants are speculators, then the stock markets are more akin to casinos.
- But, with the participation from traders, the stock markets get closer to rummy.

- However, investors take the stock markets closer to a game of bridge.
- In any case, stock markets will never become pure skill games like chess. They remain strategy games most of the time and often resemble casinos.

2. When you are at a Racecourse

If I am asked to give advice to those who are inclined to spend their time and their money on the Turf I should give them the advice 'Punch' gave to those about to marry – don't
- Archibald Primrose, 5th Earl of Rosebery

Suppose you go with a sum of $200 to bet at a racecourse. You find six horses lined up for the next race. The Table 3.2 gives

a) Track record (L : Loss, W : Win)
b) Odds offered (x-y : If you bet y, you get y+x)
c) Win Pay-offs (you win your bet amount of $ 200 plus offer)
d) Lose Pay-offs (lose your bet amount of $ 200)

Table 3.2 Track Record, Odds of Pay-offs

Horse	Track Record	Odds Offered	Win Pay-off	Loss Pay-off
Always Dreaming	LLWWWW	1-10	220	-200
I'll Have Another	WLWLWL	1-1	400	-200
Animal Kingdom	LLWWLL	6-5	440	-200
Big Brown	WWWLLL	5-1	1200	-200
Mine That Bird	WWLLLL	10-1	2200	-200
Super Saver	WLLLLL	20-1	4200	-200

We are presenting six different possible bets you may choose from.

a) bet on Super Saver, as you see that pay-off is the highest for it.
b) bet on Always Dreaming, as chances of winning are high.
c) bet on I'll Have Another, after calculating expected gain / loss.
d) bet on Big Brown because you love brown horses.
e) look around and see that many are betting on Animal Kingdom and bet on it
f) look around and see that nobody is betting on Mine That Bird and bet on it

You write down the choice number of your bet.

Go back to Table 2.1, where you have ticked against your dominant negative traits. Based on your traits, make the choice of horse again. Do the two choices tally?

Reflect why and why not the two choices are tallying or not tallying.

3. At the Roulette Table

*It's hard to walk away from a winning streak,
even harder to leave the table
when you're on a losing one*
— Cara Bertoia

Roulette Wheel and Betting Mat

A roulette wheel consists of a spinning disk with divisions that revolves around the base of a bowl. A ball is spun around the outside of the bowl until eventually the ball and the wheel come to rest with the ball in one of the divisions.

The divisions around the wheel are numbered from 1 to 36 in a seemingly random pattern alternately in red and black. Additionally, there is a green division numbered 0. At some tables, there is an extra green division marked 00.

Prior to rolling the ball, players place their bets, typically chips, on a betting mat. A sample betting mat is shown in Figure 3.1.

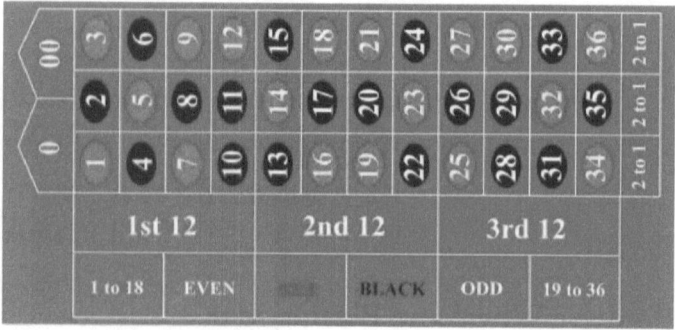

Figure 3.1 Sample Betting Mat

Roulette Bets

Much of the interest in Roulette is derived from the number of different bets that can be made and their associated odds. The basic bets are the same for all forms of modern Roulette. Below are a list of the available bets, categorized by the bet's associated odds:

(a) Even Money
- Red / Black
- Even / Odd
- Low bet (Numbers 1 – 18) / High bet (Numbers 19 – 36)

(b) 2 to 1
- First dozen : Numbers 1 - 12
- Middle dozen : Numbers 13 - 24
- Last dozen : Numbers 25 - 36
- Column bet : A column of 12 numbers

YOU, GAMES AND MARKETS

(c) Longer Odds
- 5 to 1 – Line bet : 6 Numbers
- 8 to 1 - Corner bet : 4 Numbers
- 11 to 1 - Street bet : A row of 3 numbers
- 17 to 1 - Split bet : A pair of numbers
- 35 to 1 - Straight up : A single number

Rules of the Game

Roulette is essentially a simple game to play. Once all bets have been placed using coloured chips to distinguish each player, the croupier spins the wheel and rolls the ball in the opposite direction. When the ball comes to a halt in one of the slots, the croupier announces the result, collects all losing bets and pays out the winners. The rules for Zero and Two Zeros are slightly different.

Your Strategy

a) You are at a Roulette Table with US $1,000 with you.
b) You find six people at the table.
   i. An elderly lady who appears to be a regular at the table
   ii. A middle aged couple who look serious in making money

iii. A female in her twenties apparently planning to gain experience in casino games
iv. Two gentlemen who look like faculty at the nearby mathematics university

c) You watch five rounds of the game to understand the trend.
d) The elderly lady has been betting Straight Up. She has no luck so far. In the sixth round she chooses 36.
e) The middle aged couple have also been betting Straight Up, but each on a different number. The wife wins once in the first five turns. The couple has an overall gain of 3.5 times the money they bet together.
f) The twenties odd female seems to be riding on beginner's luck. Out of the five bets she made she wins four. But all bets are on red.
g) The two gentlemen from the university have been continuously betting on the 11-1 Street Bet. One of them started from the first row 1-2-3 and moved down a row every time. The other started from the last row 34-35-36 and moved up a row every time. Neither won in the first five rounds. In the sixth round their bets are on 16-17-18 and 19-20-21.

h) In the first five rounds, the ball stopped four times on red and once on black; all five times on odd.
i) To place a bet, you need minimum US $10.
j) You have time to play a maximum of ten rounds.

Now write down your

a) first bet
b) strategy for ten rounds

In Table 2.1, you noted your dominant personality trait. Now based on the trait, write down your

a) first bet
b) strategy for ten rounds

Is there is any difference in your strategy with or without information on your trait?

4. If you were a farmer

> *Farming is a profession of hope*
> — Brian Brett

If you were a farmer in Kibamba village, Kibamba Ward in the peri-urban zone of Dar es Salaam, in Tanzania, a country in the Sub-Saharan region in the middle of the first decade of the new millennium, say 2005.

In the Sub Saharan region, agricultural sector accounted for 70% of employment, 40% of trade and 33% of GDP. The dependence of Tanzania on agricultural sector was even higher with its contribution to GDP at 45% and to the employment at 75%. Kibamba is naturally tilted towards agriculture.

As a farmer, you had to choose the crop to be sown. As there is a choice, there is a decision making process. Let us first try to put together information available with us.

Kibamba experiences seasonal rains - long rains during March to May and short rains during October to December. The long rainy season is very favourable for the cultivation of cereals like maize and not so favourable to vegetables and fruits.

The short rainy season is suitable for cultivation of vegetables and fruits, though cereals like maize need not be ruled out. If you were to decide your crop for the short rainy season then the choices can be:

- Vegetables
    o Chinese Cabbage
    o Tomato
    o Cucumber
- Root Vegetables
    o Amaranthus
    o Cassava
- Fruits
    o Banana
    o Watermelon
- Cereals
    o Maize

Let us next look at the factors that affect the decision making in the choice of a crop.

- Physical
    o Water Availability
    o Rainy Season
    o Soil Fertility
- Economic
    o Costs

- o Demand
- o Price
* Personal
  - o Individual Interest
  - o Earlier Experience
  - o Peer Preference
* Crop Profile
  - o Duration
  - o Yield
  - o Resilience to Pests
* Resources Availability
  - o Labour
  - o Fertilizers
  - o Machinery

Of the above factors, there are a few which are factual. For example, the fertility of soil, duration of the crop and availability of machinery.

However, there are some factors that need an assessment. An example of such a factor is the marketability of the crop, which requires an assessment of demand and supply at the end of the harvesting season.

Rainfall is an interesting factor. The meteorology department uses data and models to forecast rainfall. Yet, the trust in rainfall forecasts varies from individual to individual. The acceptance of forecasts is subject to the biases of the individual.

Peer preference is a factor that can act on your decisions in different ways. You can follow the choice of your fellow farmers, in the hope that they made a right choice. You may opt for another crop as you don't trust their decision making ability.

Such assessments are subjective. Biases play an important role in subjective assessments and decisions. The biases arise from individual traits.

You look at the information below to make your decision on the crop:

a) There is a general talk about shortage of maize
b) Maize requires good rainfall
c) Rainfall prediction is normal

d) You had been growing cucumber over the past five years.
e) You did not make spectacular gains, yet you made no losses either.
f) The majority of farmers started readying themselves to cultivate Chinese Cabbage
g) There has been an increasing trend in the export of tomatoes from Tanzania

h) The storage and canning facilities for tomatoes are expected to improve
i) You don't like root vegetables
j) In general, both amaranthus and cassava have continuous demand from industry

k) The coming summer is expected to be hot
l) Consumers prefer watermelon during summer
m) Demand for banana is perennial
n) Scientists came out with a new fertilizer specific to the banana crop
o) The new fertilizer is expected to increase yield of banana

p) There is a free seed and fertilizer distribution program in Kibamba
q) Your neighbour, whom you don't like at all, is as usual, waiting for your choice. He normally chooses a crop that you choose.
r) Your brother, who has as much land as you have adjacent to yours, and whom you love, depends on your advice for his choice.
s) Volunteers are around the village to give specific advice to farmers who meet them
t) There is a distant uncle of yours, who gives you unsolicited advice.

Read all information carefully. Is there any specific bias or behavioural trait that you consider can play an important role in your decision. Write it down.

Choose the crop you would sow. Give your reasons for the same.

Explain to yourself if any of your traits influenced your decision.

Was your choice to do with any one of the following questions?

- Did you continue with the crop you have been comfortable with?
- Did you choose your crop to mislead your neighbour?
- Did you opt for the crop majority started preparing to sow?
- Did you find the export opportunity news very attractive?
- Are you fed up with your uncle's advices and went against him?

5. Imagine you are an angel

> *Never go into venture capital if you want a peaceful life*
> — **Georges F. Doriot**

After running several successful businesses as a busy CEO and having lived in five continents over three decades, you retired from the active role to enjoy your life with yoga, travel, music and golf in Singapore. But you did not want your business acumen to remain underutilized and untapped by the next generation of aspirants. So you decided to wear the hat of an angel investor, which you thought would provide continued association with business and business aspirants, still leaving you with adequate leisure.

On the very first day you started your life as an angel, you received a few applications from aspiring teams of individuals, seeking your guidance and funds.

You believe that angel investors should not be philanthropists. You do philanthropy, but that is a different hat you wear. As an angel investor, your job is to pick up the right idea that has the potential to turn into a unicorn. You need to identify the right people with passion and vision. It looks simple on paper. In reality, neither the idea nor the team is time tested.

It is possible that your earlier experience and expertise can assist you in your decision making. But decisions in hitherto untested areas cannot be taken by looking at the past. They are taken based on gut feeling.

What is gut feeling? It is difficult to give a precise definition to it. The general understanding is that it is an inner voice or a sixth sense or an extra perception that enables you to foresee what is likely to happen.

As an angel investor, where availability of facts, models and analysis is not complete and comprehensive, you need to go by your gut feeling. Gut feelings may partially depend on your domain expertise and more on your emotional traits.

Let us list out the few proposals that you received:

a) Account Aggregator (AA)

Activity : Consent based collection of information and dissemination

Use Case : Convenience to customers and lending institutions in loan processing
Promoters : Three single women in mid-thirties qualified in technology and banking
Technology : Existing
Location : Singapore
Business Plan : 1000, 10000 and 100000 customers over next three years
Regulatory Stand : Clear Guidelines

b) Drone Delivery of Cash (DDC)

Activity : Cash delivery from sender to receiver through drones
Use Case : Himalayan hilly regions
Promoters : A retired banker and a retired postal department official
Technology : Drone Technology
Location : Himachal Pradesh, India
Business Plan : Cash to foreign tourists at inaccessible winter sports locations
Regulatory Stand : Government stand on drones is emerging

c) Digital Asset Auctioning (DAA)

Activity : Auctioning of digital assets like paintings, music etc

Use Case : Selling digital art
Promoters : A technologist with background in cryptos and NFT
Technology : Block Chain Technology
Location : San Jose, USA
Business Plan : Target promising digital artists
Regulator Stand : No guidelines for or against DAA

d) Teacher Student Connector (TSC)

Activity : App for connecting teachers and students
Use Case : Covid like situations where face to face teaching is not feasible
Promoters : Three teachers in Spain, France and Portugal
Technology : Available
Location : Fontainebleau, France
Business Plan : 1 million customers in two years
Regulatory Stand : No concerns

e) Virtual Traveller (VT)

Activity : Simulated flights, cars, hotels and tourist places

Use Case : Simulation of Masai Mara, Pyramids, Angkor Vat
Promoters : Two experienced travellers and two virtual reality experts
Technology : Virtual Reality
Location : Amsterdam, Netherlands
Business Plan : Target countries with travel restrictions
Regulatory Stand : No concerns

f) Old Age Day Care and Play School for Kids

Activity : Provide day care to elderly, who in turn take care of the kids
Use Case : Countries with higher aging population
Promoters : NGO working on care of elders and children
Technology : Not applicable
Location : Kyoto, Japan
Business Plan : Start small in a city and expand to other cities over 3-5 years
Regulatory Stand : Land, property and company registration

With the basic information available as above, write down your order of preference.

You managed multiple business lines in several parts of the world. You had varied experiences with different business lines and countries. They are summed up as below:

a) Among all the places you lived, you love Netherlands
b) Your success percentage in your business has been very high
c) You are not only satisfied about your success but also feel proud about it
d) As per your assessment, ladies are a better bet for new ventures
e) However, you have a negative bias against single ladies
f) Though you do philanthropy, you don't have respect for NGOs
g) You always enjoyed your trips to the Himalayas in India
h) You encouraged your employees to take a holiday for pleasure trip
i) You believe virtual classes are very poor substitutes for real classes
j) You have reservations about block chain technology, which according to you is a hype

Now with this background, will there be a change in the order of preference? Can you write down the revised order?

Compare the two. Are there any major changes?

Now, reconcile both and write down your final preference.

Write your traits that could have influenced your preferences.

6. To Lend or Not to

That's always the way in this world.
The chappies you'd like to lend
money to won't let you,
whereas the chappies you don't want to lend it to
will do everything except actually
stand you on your head
and lift the specie out of your pockets
— P.G. Wodehouse

Peer-to-Peer lending

Peer-to-Peer lending, abbreviated as P2P lending, is the practice of lending money to individuals or businesses through online services that match lenders with borrowers. P2P lending companies often offer their services online, and attempt to operate with lower overheads. They provide their services more cheaply than traditional financial institutions. As a result, lenders can earn higher returns compared to savings and investment products offered by banks. Borrowers can borrow money at interest rates lower than money lenders.

The interest rates can be set by lenders who compete for the best rate on the reverse auction model or fixed by the intermediary company on the basis of an analysis of the borrower's credit. The lender's investment in the loan is not normally protected by any government guarantee. On some services, lenders mitigate the risk of bad debt by choosing which borrowers to lend to, and mitigate total risk by diversifying their investments among different borrowers.

The lending intermediaries are for-profit businesses; they generate revenue by collecting a one-time fee on funded loans from the borrowers and by charging a borrower assessment fee from the lenders.

P2P Lending in China

Many micro loan companies have emerged in China to serve the 40 million SMEs, many of which receive inadequate financing from state-owned banks. As the Internet and e-commerce grew in the 2000s, many P2P lending platforms were founded with various target customers and business models.

By 2016 there were more than 4,000 P2P lending platforms in China, with a cash flow exceeding US $29 billion by the month of August 2016. Lender's return rate across all P2P lending platforms was about 10% per annum on average, with a few of them offering more than 24% return rate.

Some observations on the behaviour of lenders on P2P lending platforms are:

- A lender takes into account two kinds of information
- The first kind of information is about the borrower and order
- The second kind of information is about the behaviour of previous lenders
- An expert lender with judging ability takes decisions independently
- Others may imitate the behaviour of previous lenders
- Such imitating behaviour is the sign of herd behaviour

Research Study on Herd Behaviour

Renredai is a P2P lending company founded in 2010. As per the information posted by it on its website (renrendai.com), Renredai *has built a fair, transparent, stable and efficient online interactive platform for individuals with financial needs.* Users can obtain credit ratings on Renredai and issue borrowing requests to meet their individual funding needs; they can also lend their spare funds to individuals with good credit ratings through

Renredai, so as to obtain a good rate of return on their funds.

Renrendai P2P lending service platform is mainly aimed at college students, working-class and micro-business owners with good credit rating but lack of funds. The platform helps them realize their requirements such as education, home appliance purchase and entrepreneurship. For these borrowers, there is no need to furnish any collateral. Information on their identity, bank credit reports are processed by the lending platform and forwarded to the fund lender. The lender and the borrower directly reach a loan agreement.

Three researchers, Rong Liu, Ningning Chen, and Yuelei Li published a paper titled *The Herd Behaviour on Peer-To-Peer Online Lending Markets: Evidence from China* in April 2021.

The study tests the hypothesis that *herd behaviour exists in the Renrndai P2P online lending market* and concludes that there is a significant herd behaviour. The conclusion drawn from the trio is consistent with studies of other scholars. They further conclude that the herd behaviour in Renredai is partly rational, but mostly irrational.

With the above information available to you about the P2P lending, evolution of P2P lending in China and the conclusions about herd behaviour on Renredai, do you –

(a) Lend your surplus amount in Renredai P2P lending platform
(b) Borrow from Renredai P2P lending platform

What does your decision depend on – your age, your gender, your education, your profession or your financial position?

What trait of yours would have played a role in deciding to lend or borrow on Renredai?

7. Be Poker Faced

A good lawyer, just like a good poker player, must always keep his cards close to his chest
— Mallika Nawal

Poker face is a common term used to an expressionless face that hides true feelings or an inscrutable face that reveals no hint of inner thoughts. The term poker face comes from the card game of poker, which often requires a player to make other players think he is holding different cards than the ones he is actually holding. The oldest known use of the expression poker face is in the 1870s, in a book explaining the game of poker.

- Poker is a one-pack game
- The standard 52-card pack is used for Poker game
- It is suitable to any number of players from 2 to 14, but the most ideal number is 6, 7, or 8
- It is played for money, though chips are used instead of money for convenience
- Initially players place the minimum agreed bet in in the common area, called pot
- The dealer then shuffles the pack of cards and distributes the cards to all the players, one after another

- Each player sees the card and keeps them in such a way that others can't see
- After the cards are dealt and seen by players, the first round of bets start
- A player can call (place a bet), raise (increase the bet) or fold (leave the game)
- A player who folds is out of the game
- Every player has to place a bet which is at least the bet placed by the previous player
- At the end of first round, the game continues with the active players (players who have not folded)
- In the second round, each player can call or raise or fold and similarly in the subsequent rounds
- The game continues with active players left after each round
- When the last betting round has ended all active players show their cards
- The owner of the best five-card hand takes the pot
- If at any point only one active player remains, that player automatically wins the pot without having to show any cards

The objective is to win the pot, which is the aggregate of bets made by all players.

There are two ways to win.

- To have the best five-card hand at the showdown
- To persuade all the other players to fold

It is the second possibility that is interesting. If everyone believes that you probably have a good hand, then when you raise the stake, they may prefer to fold rather than add chips to the pot as they are likely to lose whatever they add to the pot. If all others fold, you win even though your hand may be worse than theirs.

It is to bluff that you have the best cards that needs a poker face on you. You should be able to make others believe you have the best possible cards.

Values / Scoring

Except in a few versions of the game, a Poker hand consists of five cards. The various combinations of Poker hands rank from Straight Flush (the highest) to No Pair or Nothing (the lowest):

- Straight Flush – A straight flush consists of five cards of the same suit in sequence, such as 10, 9, 8, 7, 6 of hearts. The highest-ranking straight flush is the A, K, Q, J, and 10 of one suit, and this combination has a special name – a royal flush or a royal straight flush. The odds on being dealt this hand are 1 in almost 650,000.

- Four of a Kind – This is the next highest hand, and it ranks just below a straight flush. An example is four aces or four 3s. It does not matter what the fifth, unmatched card is.
- Full House – This colourful hand is made up of three cards of one rank and two cards of another rank, such as three 8s and two 4s, or three aces and two 6s.
- Flush – Five cards, all of the same suit, but not all in sequence, is a flush. An example is Q, 10, 7, 6, and 2 of clubs.
- Straight – Five cards in sequence, but not all of the same suit is a straight. An example is 9♥, 8♣, 7♠, 6♦, 5♥.
- Three of a Kind – This combination contains three cards of the same rank, and the other two cards each of a different rank, such as three jacks, a seven, and a four.
- Two Pairs – This hand contains a pair of one rank and another pair of a different rank, plus any fifth card of a different rank, such as Q, Q, 7, 7, 4. Two hands that have identical pairs would be decided by the fifth

card. For example: Q, Q, 6, 6, J beats Q, Q, 6, 6, 10

- One Pair – This frequent combination contains just one pair with the other three cards being of different rank. An example is 10, 10, K, 4, 3. If two hands contain the same high pair, then the ranking of the next card in the hands determines which one wins. For example: 9, 9, 7, 4, 2 beats 9, 9, 5, 3, 2.
- No Pair – This very common hand, also called high card, contains nothing. When more than one player has no pair, the hands are rated by the highest card each hand contains, so that an ace-high hand beats a king-high hand, and so on.

Hands that are identical, card for card, are tied and the pot is split among the tied players.

Suppose you join as the eighth player at a poker table in a casino in Las Vegas. The seven players are:

- Two aged ladies, who appear to be visiting the casino regularly
- A young girl and a boy, apparently engaged to each other

- A middle aged man with a moustache, similar to that of *Hercule Poirot*
- An intelligent looking girl in spectacles, with a book on probability on her lap
- A man in his thirties, looking uncomfortable in the setup

You play four games to get a feel. You observe that -

- The two aged ladies have been poker faced throughout; though they won two games each, they did not smile
- The newly engaged couple had no clue as to what was happening, but did not care either
- *Hercule Poirot* look-alike has always been keeping grim face, raising the bet initially, but folding just after two or three rounds
- Both the intelligent looking girl and the uncomfortable looking man were folding at the earliest opportunity

Based on your observation, can you assign any negative dominant trait to each one of the players?

- Anger
- Greed
- Attachment
- Pride

- Envy
- Fear
- Pessimism
- Quixotism

In the fifth game, you got a straight flush. You know your hand is strong. The only better hand is a royal flush, which as you know has a very low probability of 1/650000.

Based on your assessment of other players, how do you proceed with the game?

(a) Keep calling without raising so that other players will continue without folding
(b) Keep raising the bet every round with a hope the pot value increases
(c) Keep acting as though you are very worried about the outcome but still calling
(d) Keep grinning giving away the strength of your cards.

8. Negative Traits and Behavioural Types

He who is not courageous enough to take risks will accomplish nothing in life
- Muhammad Ali

We identify six different types of market participant behaviour, in three classes, with a pair in each class.

The three classes are based on

- Risk stance
- Degree of independence
- Level of rational decision making

Risk stance is the amount of risk you are willing to take. Under risk stance, the pair is Aggressive and Conservative.

Degree of independence is the freedom your mind exercises in not following others. Under degree of independence the pair is Follower and Adventurist.

Rational decision making varies from totally biased to completely analytical. Under this class the pair is Analytical and Biased.

Thus, we have six market participant behaviour types, as below:

- Aggressive
- Conservative
- Follower
- Adventurist
- Analytical
- Biased

We are aware that the list above may not be exhaustive. But we feel it is sufficient to categorize market participant behaviour type, which is adequate for our book.

Let us caution that there are factors other than participant behaviour types that influence decisions. The factors may include the place, the time, the mood, the value of bet in relation to your wealth.

With this understanding, let us now try to map market participant behaviour types with negative traits we discussed in Chapter II. It is not an easy task. However, we make an attempt, because it is the core of our discussions in the book. Your behaviour in games and markets is related to your type, which itself is influenced by your trait.

It is likely that greed or anger can drive a participant to be aggressive. Attachment or envy can lead to be bias. While pride can lead a market participant to be an adventurist, fear or attachment can make one a follower.

We map market participant behaviour types to personality traits in the Table 3.3.

Table 3.3 Participant Characteristic and Influencing Personality Traits

Market Participant Behaviour Type	Personality Traits
Aggressive	Anger, Greed
Conservative	Fear
Biased	Attachment, Envy
Follower	Fear, Attachment
Adventurist	Pride
Analytical	Absence of Above

Self-Assessment

Go through the racecourse simulation game under Section 2 of this Chapter once again. See the choice of your personality trait you made.

Look at the Table 3.3 for your market participant behaviour type based on the trait. Do you agree with it?

Self-Assessment

Based on the simulated games, how do you classify yourself -

- a) Aggressive
- b) Conservative
- c) Follower
- d) Adventurist
- e) Biased
- f) Analytical

Self-Assessment

Based on discussions so far, are you a -

- a) Speculator
- b) Trader
- c) Investor

What do you like to be – speculator, trader or investor?

CHAPTER IV

Quantitative Methods

Abstract

In decision making, humans have to deal with uncertainty. Stock markets are inherently uncertain. Probability comes to help to study alternatives and chances of occurrence in uncertain circumstances. Stock market data resembles time series and stochastic processes help in modelling stock market data.

Keywords

Probability, Expectation, Variance, Standard Deviation, Correlation Coefficient, Regression Coefficient, Time Series, Stochastic Processes, Autoregressive and Moving Average Models

1. Probability

Ignorance gives one a large range of probabilities
— George Eliot

Suppose you travel back in time to the year 1654. You can watch in France a high stake game supervised by Chevalier de Méré, a philosophical gambler. Two gamblers, X and Y place 1000 gold coins each in the pot to play the game. The winner takes the pot of 2000 gold coins.

The game has five rounds. The gambler who wins a round gets one point and the gambler who gets three points first, wins the pot of 2000 gold coins. Chevalier de Méré, is the referee for the game.

At the end of three rounds X has 2 points and Y has 1 point. At this stage of game, for some unexpected reasons the game has to be stopped. As X already has 2 points, 1 more than Y, X claims 2000 gold coins. Obviously Y contests the claim of X, saying that it is possible that the next two points could be his.

Chevalier de Méré has a difficult situation to handle. He has to find a rational way of settling the dispute. Not an easy task to handle. To take the right decision, he first seeks time. Then he seeks help of two mathematician friends - Pierre de Fermat and Blaise Pascal.

The two mathematicians exchange notes with each other. Each comes up with a solution to the problem posed by Chevalier de Méré. The approach of each mathematician is different though the final result is same.

Now you know that Fermat's approach led to the concept of probability, a branch of mathematics, with applications in varied disciplines including physics, chemistry, economics, finance and medicine. Pascal's approach is the basis for the concept of expectation, a beautiful mathematical concept, applied in several fields, including finance.

We will present the solution offered by Fermat at the end of the current Section on Probability and the solution worked out by Pascal at the end of the Section 4 on Mean and Standard Deviation.

We are fully aware, that as a branch of mathematics, probability theory has a rigorous mathematical approach. However, we do not intend to discuss the axioms, definitions, notations, symbols and equations of probability theory. Our interest is limited to understanding the concept of probability intuitively, which we do through a series of examples.

Example 4.1

We know that there are six faces on a gambling dice and six numbers on each face 1,2,3,4,5 and 6. Let us assume that the dice is unbiased which means that the chances of any one of the numbers, 1 to 6, showing up are equal. As there are six numbers, we can say that the chances of occurrence of any one of them showing up is 1/6. We express chances of occurrence as a numerical fraction like 1/6, which we call as the probability of occurrence.

Example 4.2

In the game of dice, suppose we are not interested in the exact number shown up but we are interested only in knowing whether the number shown up is even or odd. As there are three even numbers out of the six numbers, we can say that chances of an even number is 3/6 = 1/2. Which means probability of even number is ½.

In our examples of rolling a dice, we have given a probability of 1/6 to each number even before we rolled the dice. Assigning probability without actually looking at the outcome, is called *a priori*.

We quite often do this. While tossing a coin, we say probability of heads or tails is 1/2 even before we toss the coin. It is another case of *a priori* probability. Such *a priori* probabilities are intuitive, not based on empirical evidence, yet very useful in practice.

However, if we are not in a position to guess the probability *a priori* then how do we find probabilities?

In case you do not know the probability of a number showing up in the case of rolling dice, you actually roll it and see. But if you roll it once, you may get one of the numbers and you cannot draw any conclusion. Even if you roll it for 6 times, you cannot draw any inference. In such cases, you have to roll the dice several times.

Example 4.3

Suppose you roll the dice 600 times. It is possible that each number 1,2,3,4,5 and 6 appears 98, 102, 99, 100, 100 and 101 times, respectively. The probability of any number showing up is the number of times it shows up by total number of rolls.

> Probability of 1
> = Number of times 1 shows up / Total number of rolls

= 98 / 600
= 0.163

Similarly the probabilities of 2,3,4,5 and 6 are 102/600, 99/600, 100/600, 100/600 and 101/600.

As these probabilities are calculated after the roll of the dice, they are called *a posteriori* probabilities. In our case, all the *a posteriori* probabilities are very close to 1/6. There does not seem to be any bias to any one number. We consider such a dice as unbiased.

Example 4.4

Suppose you roll a dice 600 times and you find that the number 1 shows up 300 times and the remaining five numbers show up 60 times each.

Probability of 1 = 300/600 = 1/2

Probability of any other number = 60/300 = 1/5

What do you understand from such a result? What is your explanation?

Let us have a look at alternative scenarios.

a) There can be a manufacturing defect or wear and tear; the dice is biased towards number 1

b) On an earlier occasion when the same dice was rolled 6000 times, the number of times each number showed up was close to 1000; so the dice is not biased

c) Events of very low probabilities do occur; it is not impossible to have 1 showing up more often than other numbers; may need more rolls to say if the dice is biased or not

Example 4.5

One way of removing the bias is to change the design.

Suppose instead of rolling a dice, you write six numbers on six pieces of paper and fold them. You pick one of the folded papers. It may be one of 1,2,3,4,5 and 6. The probability of picking any number is 1/6. Unlike a dice which can be manufactured to have a bias, or which can acquire bias over a period of time, pieces of paper may not have that kind of bias.

Example 4.6

Let us extend the folded paper example. You pick a folded paper and observe the number written on it. Let it be 4. You keep it aside and pick another folded paper. As 4 is already picked, there is no chance of picking 4. The number in the second pick can be any one of 1,2,3,5, and 6. The probability of picking any of them is 1/5. It is not 1/6 as there are only five folded papers.

Even though the process of picking folded papers is apparently similar to rolling the dice, the successive draws are not independent. The result of the second draw depends on the first draw. Similarly, the third, fourth and fifth draws depend on the previous draws.

Let us continue to see some more examples to understand the concept of probability.

Example 4.7

A card is drawn from a standard pack of 52 cards. What is the probability that it is a

a) Spades
b) Ace
c) Ace of Spades

In a pack of 52 cards, there are 13 Spades, 4 Aces and 1 Ace of Spades. Thus,

a) Probability of Spades = 13/52 = 1/4
b) Probability of Ace = 4/52 = 1/13
c) Probability of Ace of Spades = 1/52

Example 4.8

If a pair of dice is rolled, what is the probability that the sum of the two numbers is

a) 6
b) 9
c) 12

When a pair of dice is rolled, there are 36 possibilities - (1,1) (1,2) . . .. (6,6)

a) Out of the 36 possibilities, 5 result in 6 - (1,5), (2,4), (3,3), (4,2) and (5,1)
Therefore, probability of 6 = 5/36
b) Out of the 36 possibilities, 4 result in 9 - (4,5), (5,4), (6,3) and (3,6)
Therefore, probability of 9 = 4/36
c) Out of the 36 possibilities, 1 results in 12 - (6,6)
Therefore, probability of 12 = 1/36

Example 4.9

From an urn containing 3 blue, 4 red and 5 black balls, a ball is drawn randomly. What is the probability that the ball drawn is

   a) Blue
   b) Red
   c) Black

As seen earlier, the favourable number for blue, red and black are 3, 4 and 5, respectively. Since total number of balls is 12,

   a) Probability of drawing Blue = 3/12 = 1/4
   b) Probability of drawing Red = 4/12 = 1/3
   c) Probability of drawing Black = 5/12

Example 4.10

One of Chevalier de Méré's favourite bets was at least one six in a roll of dice four times. His experience was that the bet paid off more often than not.

For a change, he started betting on at least two sixes in the roll of a pair of dice twenty four times. However, he soon realized that his old approach to the game was more profitable.

YOU, GAMES AND MARKETS

He requested his friend, Pascal, the reason for the bet on one six out of four rolls of one dice yielding better results than the bet on two sixes out of twenty four rolls of a pair of dice.

Probability of at least one 6 out of 4 rolls of a dice:

- Probability of 6 in one roll = 1/6
- Probability of NO 6 in one roll = 1 − 1/6 = 5/6
- Probability of NO 6 in any one of 4 rolls = $(5/6)^4$
- Probability of at least one 6 in 4 rolls = 1 − $(5/6)^4$ = 1 − 0.4822 = 0.5177

Probability of at least 2 sixes out of 24 rolls of a pair of dice:

- Probability of 2 sixes in one roll of a pair of dice = 1/36
- Probability of NO 2 sixes in one roll = 1 − 1/36 = 35/36
- Probability of NO 2 sixes in any one of twenty four rolls = $(35/36)^{24}$
- Probability of at least 2 sixes = 1 − $(35/36)^{24}$ = 1 − 0.5086 = 0.4914

See the following rules of probability to understand the logic of some statements above. The rules may be helpful to you while attempting self-tests.

a) Every possible outcome has positive probability, however small it is. The probability can never be negative.
b) Sum of probabilities of all possible outcomes is 1; so probabilities can vary only between 0 and 1, both inclusive.
c) If the probability of occurrence of an outcome is p, then probability of it not occurring is $(1 - p)$
d) It is possible that an event with very low probability can occur, however low the probability is
e) Such events are called black swan events, made famous by Nassim Nicholas Taleb through his book titled The Black Swan

Self-Test 4.1

The first ball drawn from the urn in Example 4.9 is Black. You draw a second ball without putting the first ball back into the urn. What is the probability that the ball drawn is –

a) Blue

b) Red
c) Black

Self-Test 4.2

Do Self-Test 4.1 with the assumption, the first ball drawn is put back into the urn.

Self-Test 4.3

The range of marks in the English examination of 1000 students, as against of their mother tongues, are presented in the Table 4.1.

Table 4.1 Marks in an English Examination

Mother Tongue / Marks Range	0-50	50-60	60-70	70-80	80-90	90-100	Total
French	1253	330	438	307	138	32	2498
Spanish	977	259	344	241	109	25	1955
Chinese	1059	281	373	262	118	27	2120
Japanese	944	251	332	233	105	24	1889
Hindi	768	204	271	190	85	20	1538
Total	5000	1325	1758	1234	555	128	10000

If you pick up a student randomly, what is the probability that -

a) Mother tongue is Spanish

b) Mother tongue is neither Chinese nor Japanese
c) Marks are in the range 70-80
d) Marks are in the range 50-100
e) Marks are 90-100 with mother tongue Hindi
f) Marks are less than 50
g) Marks are less than 50 with mother tongue French

Self-Test 4.4

Find out on your own the probabilities given for each step of Example 4.10

Finally, let us look at the solution offered by Fermat to the abandoned game of Chevalier de Méré.

Fermat gave solution in terms of chances of occurrence, or probabilities. He reasoned that two more rounds would suffice to determine the winner. There are four possible outcomes, each equally likely.

The four possible outcomes are XX, XY, YX and YY.

Y wins only in the case of outcome YY. The chances of winning are, therefore, 1/4. Which means chances of X winning are 3/4 (1 − 1/4).

Thus, the ratio of chances of winning of X and Y is 3:1. Accordingly, Fermat suggested dividing 2000 gold coins in the ratio of 3:1. So

- X's share is 1500
- Y's share is 500

By this reasoning, Fermat laid the foundations of probability, which has wide range of applications.

2. Random Variable

Luck is not as random as you think. Before that lottery ticket won the jackpot, someone had to buy it
— Vera Nazarian

Experiment

An experiment is a procedure carried out under controlled conditions in order to discover an unknown effect or law, or to illustrate a known law. An experiment results in an outcome.

Example 4.11

a) Finding refractive index of glass
b) Finding specific gravity of Mercury
c) Reaction of Zinc with dilute Sulphuric Acid
d) Illustration of the presence of Carbon dioxide in the exhaled air

In all the examples of the experiment, there is only one outcome.

a) Refractive index of glass is 1.5
b) Specific gravity of Mercury is 13.6
c) Zinc reacts with dilute Sulphuric Acid resulting in Zinc Sulphate and Hydrogen

d) When exhaled air is bubbled through limewater, it leaves a milky white precipitate

There are many such experiments, where there is only one outcome which is same whenever the experiment is repeated.

Random Experiment

If an experiment has several possible outcomes, and each time the experiment is conducted the outcome can be any one of the possible outcomes, then such an experiment is called random experiment.

Example 4.12

a) Tossing of a coin – Heads or Tails
b) Rolling of a dice – Any of 1,2,3,4,5, or 6
c) Measuring temperate in a location – Can vary from minimum to maximum
d) USD-JPY Exchange rate at the opening of market in Sydney, Australia - Unpredictable

An experiment is often called a trial. As long as there is only one trial, then trial and experiment can be called interchangeably. But if an experiment involves a sequence of trials, they are not synonymous. In such cases, an experiment is considered as sequence of trials.

Example 4.13

a) Rolling a dice once; as there is only one trial, it can be called either an experiment or trial
b) Rolling a dice four times; each roll is a trial and the four trials together is an experiment
c) Tossing a coin until you get a head; each toss is a trial and all trials together is an experiment
d) Picking 3 balls from an urn of 4 White and 6 Black balls; picking a ball is a trial and picking three balls is an experiment

Among the possible outcomes, an outcome or a set of outcomes is called as an event. Event is the outcome out of a random experiment. As per our interest and requirements, we define events. Events are sub-sets of the set of all possible outcomes.

Example 4.14

a) In the case of rolling a dice, there are six possible outcomes. If our interest is only in the number, then there are six events 1, 2, 3, 4, 5, and 6.
b) However, if our interest is on whether the number is odd or even, then there are two events – Even and Odd

c) Similarly, if our interest is only to know whether the number is 6 or not 6, then there are only two events 6 and NOT 6
d) If a pair of dice is rolled, there are 36 possible outcomes. If our interest is in the sum of the two numbers, then there are 11 events and they are 2, 3, 4, 5, 6, 7, 8, 9, 10, 11 and 12.

We can assign probabilities to an outcome either *a priori* or *a posteriori*. As events are sets of outcomes, we can assign probabilities to events also. The probabilities for the events (a), (b) and (c) in Example 4.14 are -

a) Prob (1) = Prob (2) = Prob (3) = Prob (4) = Prob (5) = Prob (6) = 1/6
b) Prob (Even) = Prob (Odd) = 1/2
c) Prob (6) = 1/6

Self-Test 4.5

Calculate probabilities for all events 2 to 12 in example 4.14 (d).

Hint: When two dice are rolled, possible outcomes are 36 i.e. (1,1), (1,2) ... (1,6), (2,1), (2,2), ... (2,6) ... (6,1), (6,2), ... (6,6).

Variable

If you drop a metal ball from the top of a tower, you can calculate the time it takes to reach the ground even before you drop the ball. It will take exactly the same time as per the time-distance-acceleration relationship -

$$t = \sqrt{(2h/g)}$$

t is time ; h is height; g is gravitational force

In the equation, g is always 9.8, a constant. Time t and Height h are not constants. They are variables. Different towers have different heights. Time varies, depending on height of the tower. We can say time t is a dependent variable which depends on height h. In this equation, height h is an independent variable.

In mathematics we quite often use constants and variables. The variables used in Physics, Chemistry and other such mathematical disciplines represent what we observe in the real world around us. Therefore, those variables adhere to natural phenomenon. At the end of the experiment, they take values exactly as per laws, equations and theories behind the phenomenon.

Random Variable

Unlike the variables we use in mathematics, there are variables that exhibit random behaviour. As an example, when a dice is rolled, the number that shows up is a variable. But the variable can take any one of the values 1, 2, 3, 4, 5 or 6. The value is known only after the dice is rolled. Such variables which take values from a given set of values, but the actual value is known only after the experiment, are called random variables.

We have already seen what a random experiment is. A variable that takes a value based on the outcome of a random experiment is a random variable.

Example 4.15

a) In the experiment of rolling a dice, the random variable N, the number that shows up can take any value from 1 to 6. The value it takes is the number that shows up after the random experiment.
b) In the experiment of rolling two dice, the random variable S, sum of two numbers that show up can take any value from 2 to 12. The actual value is known only after the random experiment is conducted.

c) The rainfall in a city on a given day can be any value from zero to the maximum possible rainfall in that area. The random variable, R, can theoretically be any value from zero to infinity. The actual rainfall is the value it takes after the rainfall is recorded.

d) The opening price of Gold Fields Limited Stock on Cape Town Stock Exchange, South Africa can be any number close to the closing price of the stock price previous evening. There may be reasons for it to be much higher or lower. Opening stock price, O is a random variable. Its actual value is known after the market opens.

Self-Test 4.6

Identify which of the following are constants, variables and random variables:

a) Temperature tomorrow at 11 AM in Boston, USA
(b) Distance of Mars from Earth at 11 AM tomorrow
(c) Density of Silver in Bangkok, Thailand at 11 AM tomorrow
(d) Price of Microsoft stock on NASDAQ at 11 AM tomorrow

(e) Sum of numbers that turn up in one roll of pair of dice at 11 AM tomorrow
(f) Height of the Eiffel Tower at 11 AM tomorrow in Paris, France
(g) Resistance of a copper wire at 11 AM tomorrow in Moscow, Russia

By answering the self-test 4.5, we trust you got an intuitive idea of what a random variable is.

3. Probability Distribution

> *Whenever a large sample of chaotic elements are taken in hand and marshalled in the order of their magnitude, an unsuspected and most beautiful form of regularity proves to have been latent all along.*
> — Francis Galton

To recap the ideas discussed in the previous Section on Random Variable,

- A random experiment is an experiment with several possible outcomes and the outcome is known only after the experiment
- An outcome or a set of outcomes in which you have interest is called an event
- A random variable is a variable which takes a value based on the outcome or event of the random experiment
- As it is possible to assign probabilities to each of the possible outcomes or events, it is possible to assign probabilities to each of the values a random variable takes

For random variables N, S, R and O under Example 4.15, we can find probabilities of them taking various values indicated in the example.

Example 4.16

a) Random variable, N, takes values 1, 2, 3, 4, 5 and 6 with a probability of 1/6 each.
P (N = 1) = P (N = 2) = P (N = 3) = P (N = 4) = P (N = 5) = P (N = 6) = 1/6

b) The Table 4.2 presents the probabilities for various values that the random variable S takes. To give you an idea how the probabilities have been arrived, we show the probabilities for S = 2, 3, and 4. You can try the rest.

$$P (S = 2) = P [(1,1)] = 1/36$$
$$P (S = 3) = P [(1,2), (2,1)] = 2/36$$
$$P (S = 4) = P [(1,3), (3,1), (2,2)] = 3/36$$

Table 4.2 Random Variable, Values, Probabilities

Value	Probability
S = 2	1/36
S = 3	2/36
S = 4	3/36
S = 5	4/36
S = 6	5/36
S = 7	6/36

S = 8	5/36
S = 9	4/36
S = 10	3/36
S = 11	2/63
S = 12	1/36

c) Rainfall probabilities can be estimated from earlier rainfall data
d) Stock market opening prices can be estimated from previous stock prices, market events, company performance, etc.

Example 4.17

When an unbiased coin is tossed, it results in one of the events, Heads or Tails. Heads or Tails is not a numerical value. A random variable, by definition, takes only numerical values. In random experiments where the outcomes and events do not have numerical values, we assume numerical values to events and assign them to the random variables.

The outcomes or events of coin toss are Heads and Tails.

We define a random variable X, whose value is 1 if toss results in Heads and 0 if toss results in Tails.

Therefore, P (X = 1) = P(X = 0) = 1/2

Probability Distribution

The Table 4.2 gives probabilities for all values the random variable, S takes. Such a table giving probabilities for all values a random variable takes, is called the probability distribution of the random variable. Representation need not be in a form of a table, but can also be in the form of a function.

Let us see a few popular random variables like binomial, normal, standard normal and lognormal. Let us also see their probability distributions in a function form.

Binomial Distribution

Let an unbiased coin be tossed n times. Each toss is a trial. Each trial results in Heads or Tails. Random variable X takes value 1 if the outcome is Heads and 0 if the outcome is Tails. Now, the random experiment of trials adheres to the following conditions:

a) Each trial results in one of the two values of the variable, 1 or 0
b) Each trial is independent

c) The probability of random variable taking the value 1 is same for each trial

Such Independent repeated trials of an experiment with exactly two possible outcomes are called Bernoulli Trials.

Out of n trials, let Heads show up r times. r can vary from zero (NO Heads) to n (All Heads). Let H, the number of heads, be the random variable. We can find probabilities for each of the values H takes.

Such a random variable, which is result of a series of Bernoulli Trials, is called a Binomial Variable and its distribution is called a Binomial Distribution.

Example 4.18

Let us consider the case where n = 5. Which means the coin is tossed five times.

H can take any value from 0 (NO heads in five tosses) to 5 (ALL heads in five tosses). So we can find probabilities of H taking values 0, 1, 2, 3, 4 and 5.

Intuitively, we can find that P (H = 5) = P (ALL heads in all tosses) = $(1/2)^5$ = 0.03125

Similarly, P (H = 0) = P (NO heads in five tosses) = P (ALL tails in five tosses) = $(1/2)^5$ = 0.03125

We are not going to derive the probabilities, P (H = 1) till P (H = 4) as they involve the use of combinations and permutations of mathematics. The mathematics is quite simple. Yet we do not propose to fill the book with mathematical symbols, functions and equations.

Let us write down the probabilities for all values H takes in the Table 4.3

Table 4.3 Probability Distribution of a Binomial Variable

Value of H	Probability
0	0.03125
1	0.15625
2	0.3125
3	0.3125
4	0.15625
5	0.03125

The Table 4.3 represents Binomial Distribution with parameters n = 5 and p = ½.

You can notice from the table the following properties of a probability distribution –

a) Probabilities are assigned to all possible values the random variable can take
b) Each probability lies between 0 and 1
c) Sum of all probabilities is equal to 1

A trial need not be tossing a coin. It can be any trial that results in two complementary events. Two events are complementary to each other if the occurrence of one precludes the occurrence of the other. Let us call one event as Success and the other as Failure.

Now, we are tempted to write down the general form of distribution of a Binomial variable, even at the cost of using some symbols.

In an experiment, let us have n trials. Let probability of Success in each event be p. As we already stated p can lie between 0 and 1. Further, the probability of the complementary outcome Failure, q has to be $(1 - p)$. The probability of the random variable S taking the value r after n trials is given as -

$$P(X=r) = {}^nc_r \, p^r \, q^{(n-r)}$$

It is called the probability distribution function of the Binomial variable X.

For any probability distribution, there are two parameters that capture the behaviour of the random variable. They are mean and standard deviation. We will see them in detail in Section 4 of this Chapter. For the present let us note that

- Expectation of binomial variable is np
- Standard Deviation of binomial variable is $\sqrt{npq}$

Self-Test 4.7

Find expectation and standard deviation of the binomial variable for the following four cases.

a) n = 100, p = 0.5; r = 50
b) n = 100, p = 0.25; r = 50
c) n = 100, p = 0.75, r = 90
d) n = 100, p = 0.75, r = 25

Self-Test 4.8

For the data in Self-Test 4.7,

Find the probability of successes for each of the cases.

Normal Distribution

If you walk into a classroom and observe the heights of the students in the class, you will find that most of them are of similar height. There may be a few, very few, who are very tall or very short compared to the majority in the class.

If you find number of children in families in a locality, you will again find that they are more or less near average than they are far away from average.

Both the examples indicate that nature is somehow gifted with normality. There are abnormalities, but such abnormalities are few.

Let us look at the chart of SAT scores in the year 2020 presented in the Figure 4.1.

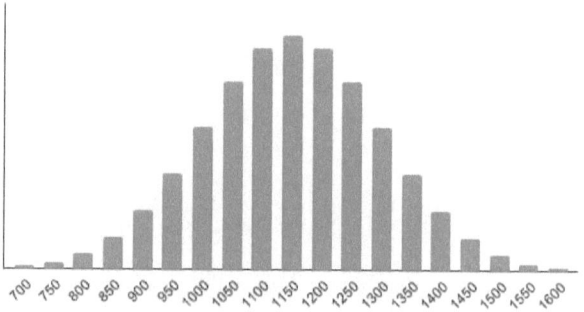

Figure 4.1 SAT 2020 Scores and Number of Students

From the Figure 4.1 you can observe the following:

- Most of the scores are in the range 950-1350, very close to the average of 1150.
- Very few scored less than 800 and very few scored more than 1500.
- The chart is not scattered, but takes a beautiful bell shape.
- The chart is symmetric around average of 1150, with equal number of students on either side.

As another example, let us look at the performances of employees in an organization as presented in the Figure 4.2.

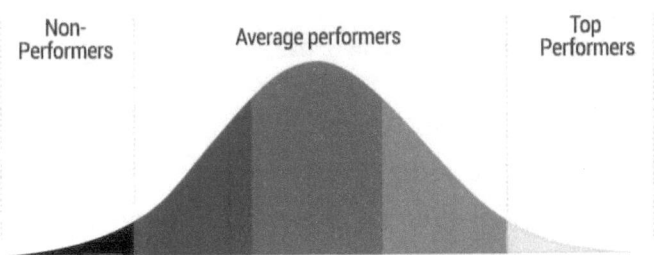

Fig 4.2 Performance of Employees

Whatever you observed in the case of SAT scores, you can observe even in the case of performance of employees.

Self-Test 4.9

Obtain data on heights in a class or number of children in families in a locality. See how the charts of such data looks. Do they resemble bell curves?

If a chart of a random variable resembles a bell curve, then the probability of the random variable taking extreme values is very low while the probability that they are close to average is high.

Such a random variable is called Normal Variable and its distribution is called Normal Distribution. Its functional form is

$$P(x) = e-(x - \mu)^2 / \sigma\sqrt{2\pi}$$

Characteristics of the Normal Variable are:

- μ is the mean
- σ is the standard deviation.
- 67% of values are between $-\mu$ and $+\mu$
- 95% between -2μ and $+2\mu$
- 99.5% of values are between -3μ and $+3\mu$
- Probability of extremes (tails), that are beyond -3μ or $+3\mu$ are less than 0.5%
- The distribution is perfectly symmetric around its mean, μ

- Probability of X < μ is equal to probability of X > μ, both equal to ½

The distribution is symmetric around mean. Yet, there can be differences in the steepness. A comparison of different steepness are given in the Figure 4.3.

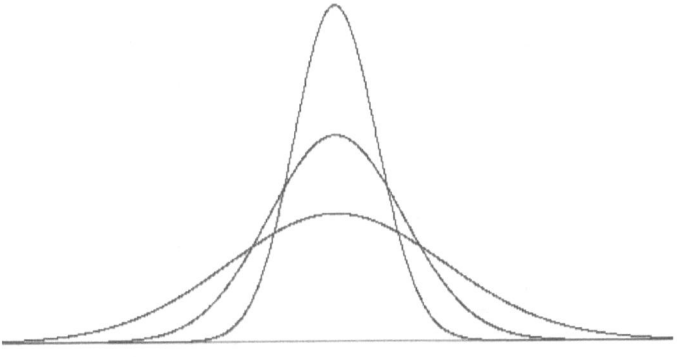

Figure 4.3 Normal Distribution with Varying Steepness

The steepness is measured by kurtosis. A kurtosis of 3 is considered neither too steep nor too flat. Curves with kurtosis equal to 3 are called playtykurtic. Curves with kurtosis greater than 3 are called leptokurtic and those with less than 3 are termed mesokurtic.

Standard Normal Distribution

μ is the location parameter and σ is the scale parameter. By subtracting μ and dividing by σ, the Normal Variable X is reduced to Standard Normal Variable, Z.

$$Z = (X - \mu) / \sigma$$

The probability distribution of Z is

$$P(z) = e{-(z)^2} / \sqrt{2\pi}$$

The probability distribution of Z looks like the graph in the Figure 4.4

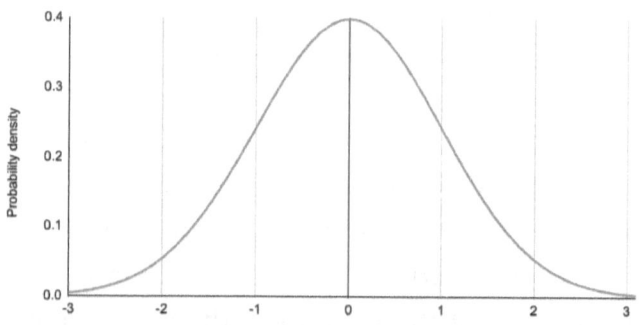

Figure 4.4 Standard Normal Distribution

Lognormal distribution

If logarithm of a random variable follows normal distribution, then the random variable is said to be following lognormal distribution. The Figure 4.5 shows the normal and lognormal distributions.

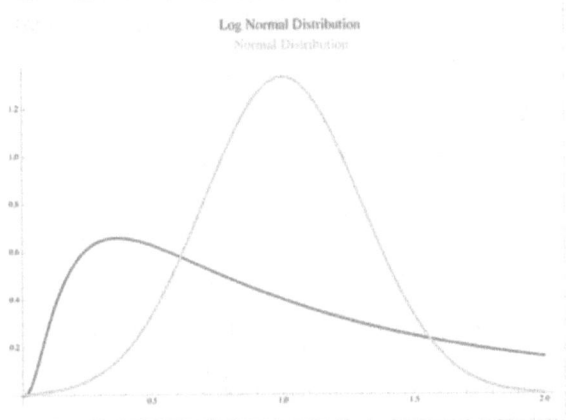

Figure 4.5 Normal and Lognormal Distribution Curves

Lognormal distribution assumes importance in valuation, especially in the Black-Scholes' option pricing model.

4. Mean and Standard Deviation

Life's under no obligation to give us what we expect
— Margaret Mitchell

If you are planning to go to Masai Mara, Kenya, one of the first inputs you would like to have is the weather condition there to decide the best period to visit. Natural attractions may look very beautiful during rains; however rains can play spoilsport to your sightseeing plans. You look at the rainfall data and you find the details of average monthly rainfall in the Table 4.4.

Table 4.4 Average Monthly rainfall in mm in Masai Mara, Kenya

JAN	FEB	MAR	APR	MAY	JUN	JUL	AUG	SEP	OCT	NOV	DEC
95	100	145	210	155	95	60	80	95	100	155	115

As you like to go when the rains are minimum, you choose July as you expect rainfall to be low during July. Your expectation is based on the past average rainfall recorded.

Based on the average, can you be sure that the rainfall in July will be only 60 mm when you visit? Can you be certain that the rainfall won't be high, as high as 210 mm, which is what you should expect in April?

Your expectation based on average does not assure you that the outcome is what you expect. It simply means that if you observe over a long period of time, on an average, the rainfall is what average indicates.

You might wonder about the utility of the concept of expectation if it cannot tell you the exact rainfall to expect. You should realize that you are not in a terrain of certainty regarding rainfall, or for that matter, temperature in a place. You have to go by averages.

Mean

It is in this context that the concept of mean comes handy. Mean gives an indication as to what you can expect in an uncertain situation. Mean is simple arithmetical average. It is easy to calculate and simple to understand. Given a set of values, mean is obtained by summing all values and dividing by the number of values.

Example 4.19

Find the mean of marks obtained by a student in six subjects: 73, 80, 100, 98, 73 and 86

Sum of the marks is 73 + 80 + 100 + 98 + 73 + 76 = 500

Mean = Sum of marks / Number of subjects = 500/6 = 83.3

Example 4.20

Sum and Mean of marks obtained by students in a class are 4000 and 80. How many students are there in the class?

Mean = Sum / Number of Students

Therefore, number of Students = Sum / Mean = 4000 / 80 = 50

Example 4.21

The pay-offs promised for five outcomes in a game of chance are given in the Table 4.5. What can be expected from the game?

Table 4.5 Pay-offs and Probabilities

Outcome	Pay-off	Probability
A	37.5	0.4
B	75	0.2
C	75	0.2

D	100	0.15
E	300	0.05
Sum	587.5	1

Sum of pay-offs is 587.5. It does not give any information about expectation. Average is sum divided by 5, which is 117.5. Interpreting it is quite tricky. A simple average is meaningful if the values have exactly the same probability of occurrence. When probabilities are different, simple average has no significance.

In such cases, weighted average of pay-offs, with weights as probabilities of realization of the pay-offs, is used. The expectation is therefore -

(sum of [pay-off X corresponding probability]) / (sum of probabilities)

The denominator, sum of probabilities, is 1.

Thus expectation is

(sum of pay-off X corresponding probability)
= 37.5 X 0.4 + 75 X 0.2 + 75 X 0.2 + 100 X 0.15 + 300 X 0.05
= 125

You can expect 125 from the game. It does not mean you will get 125 when you play the game once. It only means that if you play the game 100 times, chances of winning 12500 (100 X 125) is high.

If the cost of playing the game is anything greater than 125, say 150, you are likely to lose if you play the game 100 times, as what you expect to get by playing 100 times is 12500. Whereas, you pay 15000 to play the game 100 times.

Observations

1. Expectation is the arithmetic mean in case of a given set of values
2. In case of a random variable, it is the weighted mean of values the random variable takes, with corresponding probabilities as weights
3. Expected value is not what you can expect to get when you play the game once
4. Expected value is what you can expect to get on an average from the game if you play the game a large number of times
5. It is a very useful concept in the theory of probability

Standard Deviation

Suppose expectation from three different scenarios is same, can we have same degree of confidence in the three expectations? Let us consider an example to analyze the question.

Example 4.22

Gains and losses of three players from a game over past ten days are presented in the Table 4.6.

Table 4.6 Returns of three players from a Game

Day	Player 1	Player 2	Player 3
1	250	100	25
2	200	50	25
3	150	0	25
4	100	-25	25
5	50	-25	25
6	0	25	25
7	-50	50	25
8	-100	-25	25
9	-150	50	25
10	-200	50	25
Average	25	25	25

The average gain of each of the three players is 25. How much confidence can you have in each one of the players?

Player 3 has been consistently gaining 25 dollars. Your confidence that the Player 3 will gain 25 once again is higher than Player 2, whose gains have been inconsistent. It is possible that the Player 2 may not gain anything or even lose 25.

Though expectations from the past data, as obtained by average, is the same for both Players 2 and 3, you have a sense that Player 3 is more consistent and hence dependable. The question that naturally comes to mind is whether there is a measure of such dependability.

A measure commonly used in such cases is called standard deviation. Standard deviation is the square root of the sum of squares of deviations of each value from the mean. To understand how standard deviation can be the measure we are looking for, let us go through the process of calculating standard deviation for pay-offs of Player 2, given in the Table 4.7.

- Mean of Pay-offs is 25

- Deviation of each pay-off from mean is in the column 3.
- Average of such deviations is always zero as negative deviations and positive deviations cancel each other. Obviously we cannot use it.
- In order to overcome cancellation of positive and negative deviations, squares of deviations are calculated in the column 4.
- The average of squares of deviations from mean is called variance. 1625 is the variance.
- In order to remove the effect of squaring in terms of unit and size, square root of variance is calculated. It is called the standard deviation.
- Standard Deviation = $\sqrt{1625}$ = 40.31

Table 4.7 Calculation of Standard Deviation

Day	Pay-offs of Player 2	Deviations from Mean	Square of Deviations from Mean
1	100	75	5625
2	50	25	625
3	0	-25	625
4	-25	-50	2500
5	-25	-50	2500
6	25	0	0
7	50	25	625

8	-25	-50	2500
9	50	25	625
10	50	25	625
Average	25	0	1625

Self-Test 4.10

Find standard deviation of pay-offs of Player 3 (Hint : It may not need any calculation; just a look at the pay-offs and you may guess that the standard deviation is Zero)

Let us look at pay-offs of Player 1. There is a clear decreasing trend of pay-offs over the days. In such cases of clear trends, mean is not very meaningful. Compared to average pay-off of 25, the last five days pay-offs are 0, -50, -100, -150 and -200. Standard deviation can be calculated but it has no significance. When values exhibit a clear increasing or decreasing trend, we may not be able to use mean and standard deviation.

In all other cases, standard deviation can be a good measure of deviations of values from its mean. Higher the standard deviation, higher the deviations. Higher the deviations, lower the reliability on mean as measure of expectation.

When all the values are equal to the mean we may not need either mean or standard deviation.

As promised earlier, let us revisit the interrupted game of Chevalier de Méré. Having already seen the solution given by Fermat let us now look at the solution proposed by Pascal.

Pascal solved the problem not in terms of probabilities of occurrence but in terms of a concept, which we now call expectation. Suppose Y had already won the fourth round. In that case, the positions of X and Y would be equal, each having won two rounds, and each would be entitled to 1000 gold coins.

X should receive his portion of 1000 as he already won two rounds. Y's share of 1000, by contrast, depends on the outcome of the next round.

The next round can now be treated as a fair game for Y's stake of 1000 gold coins. Each player can expect 500, half of 1000, as chances of winning the round are equal. Hence,

- X's share is 1000 + 500 = 1500
- Y's share is 500.

It is interesting to note that the final figures obtained by Fermat and Pascal are exactly same.

Though their approaches to arrive at the figures are different. While Fermat thought through chances of occurrence, now called probability, Pascal arrived through the concept of Expectation, a key component of Probability Theory today. Both are great mathematicians, whose contribution changed the course of our understanding of uncertainty.

5. Correlation and Regression

> *Nature has established patterns originating in the return of events, but only for the most part. New illnesses flood the human race, so that no matter how many experiments you have done on corpses, you have not thereby imposed a limit on the nature of events so that in the future they could not vary.*
> — Gottfried Leibniz

We have so far been studying the behaviour of a random variable. Quite often, we have to deal with two random variables simultaneously, and sometimes even more than two.

When we look at two variables, two natural questions crop up. One. Are they related to each other? Two. Is one the cause for the other?

Let us first understand how to measure the relation between two variables. The values taken by four random variables, W, X, Y and Z are presented in the Table 4.8. Let us understand pairwise relationship between them.

Table 4.8 Variables and Correlations

W	X	Y	Z
1	2	10	14.56
2	4	9	145.80
3	6	6	4.69
4	8	7	236.94
5	10	6	890.87
6	12	5	531.84
7	14	4	511.26
8	16	3	648.44
9	18	2	258.92
10	20	1	-482.17

Relation between W and X

The values clearly indicate that if X increases Y also increases. They also indicate that if X goes up by 1 unit, Y goes up 2 units, uniformly. You can easily infer that X and Y are related, strongly related, strongly positively related.

Relation between W and Y

The values clearly indicate that if X increases, Z decreases. They also indicate that if X goes up by 1 unit, Z goes down by 1 unit, uniformly. You can easily infer that X and Y are related, strongly related, strongly negatively related.

Relation between W and Z

It is apparent from the table that the values Z takes has no relation at all to the values W takes.

Correlation Coefficient

Correlation coefficient is a measure of the relationship between two variables. Correlation coefficient between two variables X and Y is defined as covariance between the variables divided by the product of standard deviations of each variable. Correlation coefficient is usually denoted by the Greek letter ρ. The formula for ρ is

$$\rho(X,Y) = Cov(X,Y) / \sigma_X \sigma_Y$$

Cov (X,Y) is the average of products of deviations of the observations from their respective means.

Deviations of some observations from mean would be positive while the others would be negative.

If two variables move in the same direction, then the deviations of observations from respective means will have the same sign either positive or negative. Thus, the product of deviations is positive. So, the covariance, which is the average of products, is also positive.

If the variables move in opposite direction, then the signs of deviations from the respective means would have opposite signs. In such a case, the product of deviations is negative. Hence, the covariance which is the average of the products, is also negative.

Covariance has two drawbacks:

- Covariance is a large number for easy interpretation or comparison
- As a product, its unit is the product of units of the two variables

To overcome the problem of size and units, covariance is divided by the product of standard deviations. The resultant is called Correlation Coefficient.

Properties of Correlation Coefficient, ρ, are:

- Is a pure number without any units
- Always lies between -1 and +1
- Variables are positively related if $\rho > 0$, strongest when it is 1
- Variables are negatively related if $\rho < 0$, strongest when it is -1
- Variables are not related when $\rho = 0$

Self-Test 4.11

Look closely at the observations of random variables W, X, Y and Z in Table 4.6. Look at the correlation coefficients between W and X, W and Y and W and Z. They are 1, -1 and 0. Verify the result either intuitively or through calculations.

Example 4.23

A few pair of variables that may not be correlated with each other are-

- Coffee Consumption and IQ
- Height and Exam Scores
- Shoe Size and Movies Watched

Example 4.24

Scatter diagrams help in getting a fairly good idea of correlation coefficients. See the Figure 4.6 to understand the shape of a scatter diagram and the correlation coefficient.

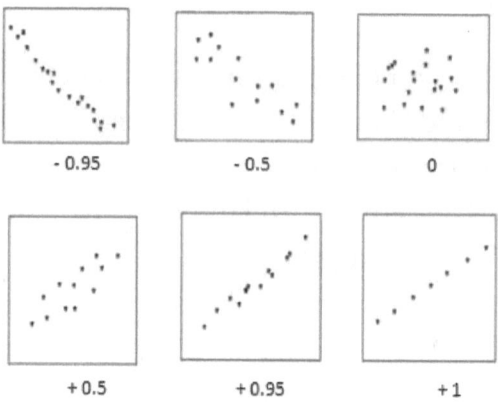

Figure 4.6 Scatter Diagrams and Correlation Coefficients

Self-Test 4.12

Write pairs of variables that are (a) positively correlated and (b) negatively correlated.

Regression Coefficient

The concept of Correlation Coefficient is very helpful in understanding the relationship between two variables. Correlation Coefficient not only tells whether two variables are related to each other, but also tells whether they are positively related or negatively related. Further it tells the strength of the relationship.

However, correlation does not imply causation. Quite often, there is a common underlying variable that moves two variables together. The best example of such a variable is time. Over time, many economic variables move up. It is not necessary that one of the economic variables influences the other.

Let us see a few pairs of variables where causation is clear from one variable to another. Rainfall influences agricultural production. The causation is one way. It is from rainfall to agricultural production and not from agricultural production to rainfall. Similarly, cholesterol levels can impact heart ailments and higher tourist inflow can increase hotel rents.

We can have an intuitive idea of the causation. But we may not be able to assess the direction and dimension of the causation. Regression Coefficient helps us in measuring the sign and strength of causation.

When we define Correlation Coefficient between two variables X and Y, the order of X and Y does not matter. But to define Regression Coefficient, we need to take into account the causal (independent) and resultant (dependent) variables. If X causes Y then we define regression coefficient as Y on X. We denote regression coefficient Y on X as $r_{Y/X}$.

Regression Coefficient $r_{Y/X}$ is obtained by dividing covariance between X and Y by variance of X.

Properties of regression coefficient $r_{Y/X}$:

1. If $r_{Y/X} > 0$, then as X goes up Y also goes up
2. If $r_{Y/X} < 0$, then as X goes up Y goes down
3. In either case, the movement of Y is $r_{Y/X}$ times the movement of X

On the other hand, if Y causes X then we define regression X on Y and denote Regression Coefficient as $r_{x/y}$. Regression Coefficient of X on Y, $r_{X/Y}$ is obtained by dividing the covariance between X and Y by the variance of Y. Properties of $r_{x/y}$ are similar to $r_{Y/X}$.

6. Random Sampling

> *Friendship is a totally biased sample of the population: we only pick out the best ones*
> — Victor Bello Accioly

Population

A population is the entire group that you want to draw conclusions about. In other words, a population is any collection of persons or objects or events in which you are interested.

Sample

A sample is a subset of a population.

Example 4.25

100 bottles of a medicine in a carton at a pharmacy is population. 2 bottles out of 100 is a sample.

Example 4.26

1000 students in a school is population. 25 students out of 1000 is a sample.

Random Sample

A random sample is a subset of a population, where each member of the sample is selected randomly, without any bias for any member of the population. A random sample, where the probability of selecting any member of the population is equal, is called a simple random sample. 4.27 and 4.28 are examples of simple random samples.

Example 4.27

Pick two bottles from the carton, without looking into the carton; without any bias for selecting any one bottle. The probability of picking up a bottle is equal for all bottles and is equal to 1/100. The selected two bottles is a simple random sample.

Example 4.28

Write down Student IDs of all 1000 students on pieces of paper, fold them and put them in a bag. Pick 25 folded papers and note down the IDs and names of the 25 students. The selected sample is a simple random sample.

Observation

Member of a sample is called as an observation.

Example 4.29

The two bottles picked from the carton are two observations.

Example 4.30

The 25 students selected at random from a school are 25 observations.

Observation Value

An observation has multiple features. While selecting a sample, you have some specific interest in one of the features. You measure the value of that feature and that value is called the observation value. It is usually a number.

Example 4.31

In the case of bottles, you may be interested in the weight of the bottle. If the weights of the two bottles selected from the carton are 9.99 gms and 10.01 gms, then they are the observation values.

Example 4.32

While selecting students in a class you may be interested in their marks. Marks of 25 students like (98, 89, 45, 32, . . . 76) are the observation values.

Independent Observations

An observation is independent if its value is not dependent on other observations.

Example 4.33

The weight of a bottle is not dependent on the weights of the other bottles. So the observations are independent.

Example 4.34

Height, weight or marks of a student in a school does not depend on height, weight or marks of other students. They are independent.

Features of Simple Random Sample

- Observations are independent
- Order of observations is not important

7. Time Series and Stochastic Processes

Quantum theory provides us with a striking illustration of the fact that we can fully understand a connection though we can only speak of it in images and parables
— Werner Heisenberg

Time Series

A time series is a series of observations of a variable at different points of time. It differs from simple random sample because -

- Observations are not necessarily independent; usually they are not
- Order is important; observations are sequenced as per time

Example 4.35

Daily sales of cars in a year in a country

Example 4.36

Average annual rainfall in a city over a century

Discrete Time Series

A time series is discrete when observations are taken only at specific times, usually equally spaced, even if the measured variable is a continuous variable.

Example 4.37

Hourly temperature of a patient during a day

Example 4.38

Daily closing price of Apple stock during a quarter

Continuous Time Series

A time series is continuous when observations are made continuously through time, even when the measured variable can only take a discrete set of values.

Example 4.39

Temperature at Beijing airport

Example 4.40

Distance travelled by a space craft

Deterministic Time Series

A deterministic time series is one which can be expressed explicitly by a mathematical expression.

It has no random or probabilistic aspects. Its past and future can be completely specified by suitable mathematical formulas. You can state how it behaved in the past and also predict how it behaves in the future.

Example 4.41

If a hot object of $100^0 C$ is left in a room, its temperature decreases as per the law of cooling. The temperatures observed once every two minutes follow the law. The observed temperature time series is deterministic.

Example 4.42

The value of an asset doubles every five years. If the original investment is 100,000 then it becomes 200,000 at the end of five years, 400,000 at the end of ten years and so on.

Non-Deterministic Time Series

A nondeterministic time series is one which cannot be described by a mathematical expression. It is inherently random in nature and does not support a mathematical expression.

Example 4.43

Average annual Rainfall in Mumbai, India during 1901-2021

Example 4.44

Weekly inflation figures in Turkey during 2021

Since nondeterministic time series have a random aspect, they are modelled using probabilistic or stochastic processes.

Stochastic Process

A stochastic process is a collection of random variables indexed by the variable t, representing time.

Example 4.45

Temperature of a furnace in a factory is measured every minute from 9 AM to 5 PM.

There are in all 480 observations of temperature at time points 9.00, 9.01 and so on.

In the case of a random variable, we can repeat the experiment and observe a different value for each repetition. In the case of a stochastic process, the experiment at a specific time point cannot be repeated. The value at that time point is the only observation available. However, as we measure the value of the random variable at different time points we have the set of observed values. The set of observations is called the realization of the stochastic process.

Example 4.46

Monthly rainfall in Mumbai, India over 10 years.

There are 120 observations; 12 observations for each year. The set of 12 values in each year is a realization. As you have values for 10 years, you have 10 realizations of the stochastic process, each realization being a set of 12 values.

By now, you would have understood that what is available to study a stochastic process is just a set of observations, called the realization. You naturally would doubt if it is possible to model a stochastic process with the availability of just one realization.

In this context, we can assure you that it is possible to model stochastic processes and use the model to forecast future. It is possible because there are interesting types of stochastic processes possessing very "nice" properties. We introduce to the readers a few interesting processes and models.

Stationary Process

A stochastic process is stationary if

a) mean is constant over time
b) variance is constant over time
c) covariance depends only on the time lag (covariance between X_t and X_{t-k} depends only on k)

A stationary process has a mean reverting tendency. Mean may move up and down; but it does not stray away; it keeps coming back to the long-term average. There is discipline in stationary processes.

In view of the discipline in the stationary process, it is possible to model it for forecasting. Autoregressive and Moving Average models are used for forecasting stationary processes.

Models for Forecasting

An Autoregressive (AR) model is one where the current value is expressed in terms of previous values and a residual term. An AR model which uses just the immediately previous value is called AR (1). An AR model that uses previous m values is called AR (m).

Moving Averages (MA) model is one where the current value is expressed in terms of the past residual terms. A MA model that depends on just one previous residual term is MA (1). MA (n) considers the previous n residual terms.

ARMA (m,n) considers previous m values and earlier n residual terms.

However, AR, MA and ARMA models can be used provided the process is stationary.

Difference Stationary

If a time series is not stationary, it can be made stationary by differencing. Differencing is the process of deriving a new series as difference between two consecutive values of the original series.

Normally a series becomes stationary by differencing the original series once. However, if the differenced series is not stationary, the differencing process has to continue. The number of times differencing is required to get stationary series is called the order of differencing.

Once the stationary series is derived after an order of differencing of p, ARMA model can be applied on it. The model is called ARIMA (m,p,n).

8. Tying Knots

It's a cruel and random world, but the chaos is all so beautiful
— Hiromu Arakawa

We have spent enough time on Quantitative Methods in this chapter. You may be wondering about their relevance to stock markets. Let us now tie the knots between the quantitative methods we learnt so far and their applications in stock markets.

Expectation and Return

Suppose you are considering to buy a stock in the automobile sector. You have narrowed your choice between Honda and Toyata. You want to know what to expect from an investment from each. Your time horizon of investment is 20 years. The Table 4.9 gives annual returns of the two stocks for 20 years.

Table 4.9 Annual Returns of Toyata and Honda

Year	Toyata	Honda
2021	19.88%	0.71%
2020	9.98%	-0.21%
2019	21.07%	7.03%
2018	-8.72%	-22.39%

2017	8.51%	16.75%
2016	-4.75%	-8.58%
2015	-1.94%	8.16%
2014	2.92%	-28.61%
2013	30.75%	11.94%
2012	41.01%	20.92%
2011	-15.90%	-22.66%
2010	-6.57%	16.52%
2009	28.61%	58.86%
2008	-38.36%	-35.61%
2007	-20.95%	-16.19%
2006	28.38%	36.49%
2005	27.79%	11.17%
2004	19.08%	15.82%
2003	29.72%	24.58%
2002	4.00%	-11.37%
2001	-19.05%	10.33%
Mean	7.4%	4.4%

Expected returns are obtained as simple averages. The expectation from Toyata at 7.4% is higher than the expectation from Honda at 4.4%.

Standard Deviation and Risk

To invest in stocks, we cannot just rely on return. We also need to see the risk associated with the return. A measure of risk is standard deviation.

For the data in the Table 4.9, the expected return on Toyata is higher than that on Honda. Let us look at the risks by calculating the standard deviations of stocks.

- Standard Deviation of Returns from Toyata = 0.205
- Standard Deviation of Returns from Honda = 0.221

The risk, as measured by standard deviation, is lower for Toyata compared to Honda. Normally higher return is associated with higher risk. But in our example, Toyata carries higher return with lower risk – very unusual, but attractive scenario.

Regression Coefficient and Systematic Risk

When you want to add a new stock into your existing portfolio, you select stocks with higher return and lower risk. Further you also select stocks whose returns move in opposite directions to the existing stocks in your portfolio. The idea is that if the return on one of the stocks in your existing portfolio moves down, then the return on the new stock moves up, thus ensuring your overall portfolio return does not fall drastically.

The process of building a portfolio with stocks having movements in the opposite directions is called diversification. To know whether the returns of two stocks move together or opposite, you can use the concept of Correlation Coefficient. You know that two stock returns move in opposite directions if Correlation Coefficient is negative.

Example 4.47

An example of such an investing is a café and an ice cream parlour in a hill station during summer. Sales of both coffee and ice cream depend on rainfall, but in opposite directions. If it rains heavily in the hill station, cafe gets high returns. However, if there are no rains in the hill station, the ice cream parlour is a good option. But as you do not know whether it would rain or not, it is a good idea to invest in both cafe and parlour. The question of how much in each is a problem to be solved using optimization techniques.

Whatever be the percentage you invest in each stock, the overall return is less than the one with higher return. Though return of portfolio lies between returns of individual stocks, the risk of the portfolio is less than the risk of each of the stocks. As your aim of diversification is to minimise the overall risk, you settle for a lower return, in order to reduce the risk.

Therefore, as more stocks are added to the portfolio, the risk of the portfolio decreases. Researchers and practitioners have found that a portfolio, however well it is diversified, still has an element of risk. It is evident from the risk observed in stock market indices. An index like S&P 500 or Dow is a highly diversified portfolio as it includes several stocks traded on the exchange. There is still a risk in investing in an index.

The risk inherent in the market is called systematic risk, which cannot be reduced by diversification. As you cannot reduce risk of a portfolio beyond a level by diversification, all that you can do is to compare your portfolio return with that of the market. Regression Coefficient is that measure which tells you how the returns of your portfolio fare vis-a-vis market.

Regression coefficient between your portfolio returns and market returns gives a measure of sensitivity of your portfolio returns to changes in market returns. Let us look at two hypothetical portfolios H1 and H2 and compare their returns with Dow Industrial Average return. The Table 4.10 gives data on returns from the Dow and the two hypothetical portfolios.

Table 4.10 Returns from Dow, H1 and H2

Day	Dow Return	H1 Return	H2 Return
Jan 21, 2022	-0.01296	-0.01944	-0.00648
Jan 20, 2022	-0.00894	-0.01341	-0.00447
Jan 19, 2022	-0.00961	-0.01441	-0.0048
Jan 18, 2022	-0.01513	-0.02269	-0.00756
Jan 14, 2022	-0.00559	-0.00838	-0.00279
Jan 13, 2022	-0.00487	-0.0073	-0.00243
Jan 12, 2022	0.001056	0.001585	0.000528
Jan 11, 2022	0.005078	0.007617	0.002539
Jan 10, 2022	-0.00449	-0.00674	-0.00225
Jan 07, 2022	-0.00013	-0.0002	-0.000066
Jan 06, 2022	-0.00469	-0.00703	-0.00234
Jan 05, 2022	-0.01067	-0.016	-0.00533
Jan 04, 2022	0.005866	0.008798	0.002933
Jan 03, 2022	0.006791	0.010186	0.003395

We can calculate the regression coefficients of returns of H1 and H2 on the returns of Dow. They are 1.5 and 0.5. How do we interpret these regression coefficients?

A regression coefficient of 1.5, which is greater than 1 indicates that portfolio H1 is aggressive compared to Dow. If Dow moves up by 1 then the portfolio moves up by 1.5. It looks attractive. But if Dow moves down by 1, the portfolio moves down by 1.5.

Returns of portfolio H2, with regression coefficient of 0.5, move up or down half that of the movements of Dow. The portfolio gains or losses are less than Dow. It is a defensive portfolio.

Thus, regression coefficient measures the risk of a portfolio; higher the regression coefficient riskier the portfolio.

Normal Distribution and Stock Returns

The assumption behind most of the financial market theories, which we will discuss later in Chapter V, is that the stock returns follow normal distribution. You may recollect the following properties of normal distribution:

- μ is the mean

- σ is the standard deviation.
- 67% of the values are between - μ and + μ
- 95% of the values are between -2 μ and +2 μ
- 99.5% of the values are between -3 μ and +3 μ
- Probability of extremes (tails), that are beyond -3 μ or +3 μ are less than 0.5%
- The distribution is perfectly symmetric around its mean, μ
- Probability of X < μ is equal to probability of X > μ, both equal to 1/2

The properties of Normal Distribution are so beautiful, that there is a temptation to use it anywhere, including stock market returns. But we can't superimpose a distribution on a random variable unless there is empirical evidence to do so. Fortunately, researchers have been finding that stock market returns follow Normal Distribution.

For stock market returns to follow Normal Distribution, the following assumptions have to be fulfilled:

- Market Participants behave rationally
- They take decisions based on data and analysis

- Data on markets is available to all participants
- Participants do not go by their individual idiosyncrasies

Though there are critics of the above assumptions, especially rationality of market participants, normal distribution for stock returns is widely accepted and used. It works in most of the cases except during black swan events.

Time Series and Stock Market Data

Stock price and its return are random variables, whose values are known only after they are realized.

Depending on individual interest, stock prices are available at different intervals.

- For an intra-day trader, tick data is available almost every moment of the day
- For a short term speculator, day end data is available every day
- For a long term investor, data over months and years is available

Typically, stock market data is a time series. Data is available at different points of time, at periodical and regular intervals.

The unique characteristic of any time series data is that there is only one realized value. As stock market data is a time series it also has only one realized value. It is a typical stochastic process. However, stock prices are not stationary. But they are difference stationary i.e the series obtained as differences between two stock prices is stationary. Interestingly differences between two stock prices are stock returns. Thus stock returns is a stationary stochastic process. Stationary stochastic processes are amenable to autoregressive and moving average models.

Stochastic Process and Modelling Stock Returns

We have seen that models like AR, MA and ARMA can be used only for stationary time series. We have also seen that stock returns, which are the differences between successive stock prices are stationary, though stock prices themselves may not be stationary.

All models like AR, MA and ARMA are used to model stock returns data. The models are also used for forecasting purposes.

CHAPTER V

Stock Market Theories

Abstract

Technical Analysis and Fundamental Analysis have been used for studying stocks while taking buy and sell decision. Models like Capital Asset Pricing and Arbitrage Pricing have also been in use. Random Walk Theory and Efficient Market Hypothesis state that it is not possible to beat markets consistently. Keynes discussed Animal Spirits, which to some extent is the forerunner to the behavioural finance theories decades later.

Keywords

Charts, Trends, Patterns, Waves, Ratios, Random Walk, Efficient Market, Beta, Bounded Rationality, Prospect Theory, Nudge Theory, Greater Fool Theory

1. Dow and Technical Analysis

Events seem to be ordered into an ominous logic
— Thomas Pynchon

Technical analysis is the study of stock price graphs. It is based entirely on stock prices and their movements. The analysis does not consider the study of financial statements of the company, which include balance sheet, profit and loss account, cash flows statement and related ratios. Such a study is part of fundamental analysis, which we will discuss in Section 2 of this Chapter.

The assumptions for technical analysis are:

a) Stock prices reflect everything; including fundamentals
b) Market considers only price movements; price movements follow trends
c) Trends repeat themselves; strategies can be based on trends

Dow Theory

The Dow Theory on stock price movement is a form of technical analysis. The theory was derived from 255 wall street journal editorials written by Charles H Dow, journalist, founder and first editor of the Wall Street journal and co-founder of Dow Jones and company.

Dow Theory is based on the hypothesis that the stock market does not behave randomly. Rather, it is guided by some specific trends. Dow Theory identifies three types of trends – Primary Trend, Secondary Trend and Minor Trend.

Primary trends last a year or more. They may be bullish or bearish. Within broader primary trends there are secondary trends, often working against the primary trend, such as a pullback within a bull market or a rally within a bear market. These secondary trends may last from three weeks to three months. Finally, there are minor trends lasting less than three weeks, which are largely noise.

In addition to the above general assumptions of technical analysis Dow Theory assumes the following:

a) Market price is determined by demand and supply forces
b) Prices move in trend for long periods
c) Reversal or shift in price trends may occur
d) Charts and graphs can predict change in demand and supply forces

Charting is the basic tool for identifying price trends based on historical data. Charts are drawn for an individual stock or market or for both. They are drawn for both price and volume. The trends are used to forecast future behaviour. We will see a few charts like bar charts and line charts to get an understanding of how they are drawn and used.

Elliot Wave Theory

The theory was developed by Ralph Nelson Elliot. According to the theory, stock price movements can be predicted because they move in repeated up-and-down patterns called waves. The waves are created by investor psychology or sentiment.

The theory identifies two different types of waves: motive waves and corrective waves. A motive wave is a price movement in the direction of the main trend. In other words, each motive wave is a step forward during a rally. As the name implies, a corrective wave comes after a motive wave. So, during a trend, motive and corrective waves form one after the other. While a motive wave is a move forward, a corrective wave is a step back within a trend.

The motive and corrective waves are nested in a self-similar fractal to create larger patterns. For example, a one-year chart may be in the midst of a corrective wave, but a 30-day chart may show a developing motive wave. A trader with this interpretation of Elliot waves may thus have a long-term bearish outlook with a short-term bullish outlook.

Interestingly, Elliott recognized that the number of waves in motives and correctives are represented by Fibonacci Series. Further, wave relationships in price and time also exhibit Fibonacci ratios, such as 38% and 62%.

Having seen Dow and Elliot theories, let us now look at charts that are used in technical analysis. Charts are drawn giving opening, high, low and closing prices. Volumes are indicated in the charts. As examples, let us see bar chart and line chart.

Bar Chart

Bar Chart is a popular technique of showing the price variation and volume on a particular day.

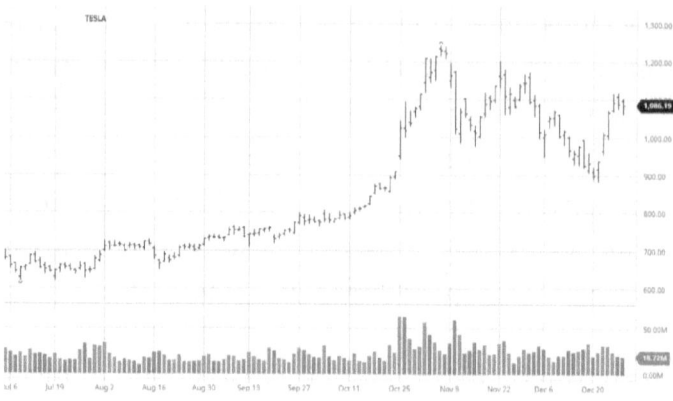

Figure 5.1 Bar Chart for Tesla Stock

The chart is made up of a series of vertical lines that represent each data point. Each vertical line represents the high and low for the trading period, along with the closing price. The closing price is indicated by a horizontal dash. The Figure 5.1 is the bar chart of Tesla stock.

Line chart

Line chart shows closing price of a stock over a set period of time. It does not provide the information of high, low and opening prices. Volumes are represented as they are done in bar charts. The Figure 5.2 is line chart for Apple Stock.

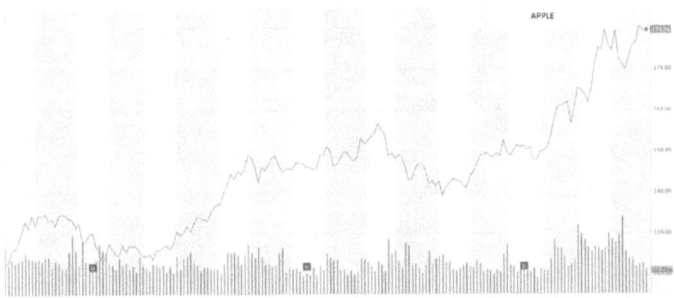

Figure 5.2 Line Chart for Apple Stock

There are several other charting techniques like Point and Figure Chart and Candlestick Chart.

Before we end our discussion on technical analysis theories, let us see some concepts that help in selling and buying strategies. Levels and Patterns are usually used in this regard.

Levels

There are two important levels to be watched – support and resistance. Support is the price level at which demand is thought to be strong enough to prevent the price from declining further. Resistance is the price level at which supply is thought to be strong enough to prevent the price from rising further. The Figure 5.3 shows the support and resistance levels in a chart.

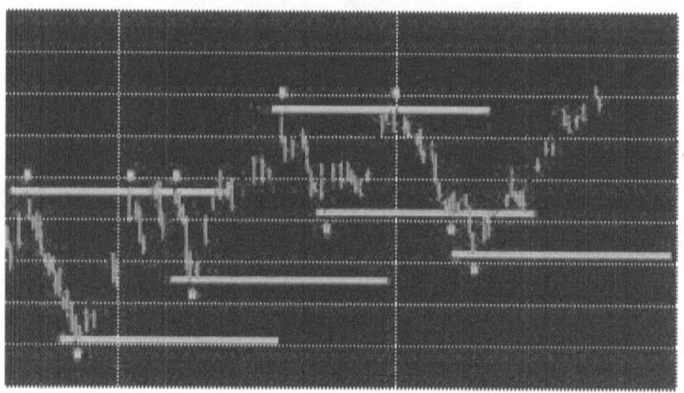

Fig 5.3 Support and Resistance Levels

The Table 5.1 gives a summary of the inclination of buyers and sellers as prices tend towards support and resistance levels.

Table 5.1 Inclinations at Support and Resistance Levels

	Declines towards Support	Advances towards Resistance
Buyer	More Inclined to Buy	Less inclined to Buy
Seller	Less inclined to Sell	More inclined to Sell

Patterns

Observing patterns helps in understanding the continuation or reversal of trends. The continuation patterns suggest that there is only a pause in the market and the old trend will continue again after the pause. The reversal patterns are those which indicate a reversal of the existing trend. The Figure 5.4 shows different shapes of reversal and continuation patterns.

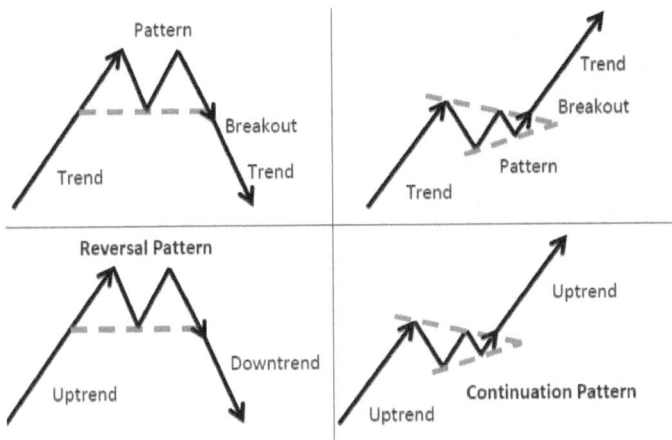

Figure 5.4 Reversal and Continuation Patterns

The Table 5.2 gives a summary of market strategies when continuation and reversal patterns are observed for increasing and decreasing trends.

Table 5.2 Strategies for Continuation and Reversal Patterns

	Increasing	Decreasing
Continuation	Hold and Don't Sell	Wait and Don't Buy
Reversal	Sell	Buy

2. DuPont and Fundamental Analysis

Focus on Return on Equity; Not Earnings Per Share
- Warren Buffet

Technical Analysis helps you garner quick short term returns. It helps you time the market for a better entry and exit. However, it may not be a very effective approach to create wealth. Wealth is created by making intelligent long term investments.

Fundamental Analysis is to study a company to invest in its stock. When an investor wishes to invest in the stock of a company for long term, say 3 to 5 years, it becomes extremely essential to understand the company from various perspectives. It is critical for an investor to separate the daily short term noise in the stock prices and concentrate on the underlying business performance. Over the long term, stock prices of a fundamentally strong company tend to appreciate, thereby creating wealth for its investors.

However, both Technical Analysis and Fundamental Analysis must coexist in your market strategy.

The fundamental analysis is basically based on the annual report of the company. There are both quantitative and qualitative aspects to be looked in the annual report to understand the fundamentals of a company.

A typical annual report contains the following sections:

- Financial Highlights
- The Management Statement
- Corporate Information
- Directors' Report
- Report on Corporate Governance
- Financial Statements

As you would agree, the financial statements are perhaps one of the most important aspects of an Annual Report. There are three financial statements a company will present namely:

- The Profit and Loss statement
- The Balance Sheet
- The Cash flow statement

The profit and loss statement presents revenue details of the company, the expenses incurred to generate the revenues, tax and depreciation and the earnings per share, The balance sheet gives details of assets, liabilities and shareholders' equity. The cash flow statement reveals how much cash the company is actually generating.

Financial Ratios Theory

The best way to study the financial statements is by studying the financial ratios. The theory of financial ratios was made popular by Benjamin Graham, who is popularly known as the father of fundamental analysis. Financial ratios help in interpreting the results, and allows comparison with previous years and peer-companies.

For analyzing the position of a company, the financial ratios can be classified into different categories. The classification is somewhat loose as there are overlapping interpretations. Ratios, irrespective of the category they belong to, convey a certain message, related to the financial position of the company. Thus, even a loose classification is good enough for us.

The four categories are:

- Profitability Ratios
- Leverage Ratios
- Operating Ratios
- Valuation Ratios

The Profitability Ratios help you measure the profitability of the company. The ratios convey how well the company is able to perform in terms of generating profits. Profitability of a company also signals the competitiveness of the management. As the profits are needed for business expansion and to pay dividends to its shareholders a company's profitability is an important consideration for the shareholders. A few Profitability Ratios are:

- EBITDA Margin (Operating Profit Margin)
- PAT Margin
- Return on Asset (RoA)
- Return on Capital Employed (RoCE)
- Return on Equity (RoE)

The Leverage Ratios, also referred to as Solvency Ratios / Gearing Ratios, measure the company's ability to sustain its day to day operations. Leverage ratios measure the extent to which the company uses the debt to finance growth. They also help in understanding the company's long-term sustainability, keeping its obligation in perspective. Some important Leverage Ratios are:

- Interest Coverage Ratio
- Debt to Equity Ratio
- Debt to Asset Ratio
- Financial Leverage Ratio

The Operating Ratios, also called the Activity Ratios, measure the efficiency at which a business can convert its assets to revenues. This ratio helps us understand how efficient the management of the company is. For this reason, Operating Ratios are sometimes called the Management Ratios.

- Fixed Assets Turnover Ratio
- Working Capital Turnover Ratio
- Total Assets Turnover Ratio
- Inventory Turnover Ratio
- Inventory Number of Days
- Receivable Turnover Ratio

The Valuation Ratios compare the stock price of the company with either the profitability of the company or the overall value of the company to get a sense of how cheap or expensive the stock is trading. Thus, these ratios help us in analyzing whether the current share price of the company is perceived as high or low. In simple words, the valuation ratios compare the cost of a security with the perks of owning the stock.

- Price to Sales (P/S) Ratio
- Price to Book Value (P/BV) Ratio
- Price to Earnings (P/E) Ratio

P/E Ratio

The price-to-earnings ratio or P/E ratio is one of the most widely used stock analysis tools by which investors and analysts determine stock valuation. In addition to showing whether a company's stock price is overvalued or undervalued, the P/E can reveal how a stock's valuation compares to its industry group or a benchmark like the S&P 500 Index.

In essence, the P/E indicates the dollar amount an investor can expect to invest in a company in order to receive US $1 of that company's earnings. This is why the P/E is sometimes referred to as the price multiple because it shows how much investors are willing to pay per dollar of the earnings. If a company is currently trading at a P/E of 20, the interpretation is that an investor is willing to pay US $20 for US $1 of the current earnings.

The P/E ratio helps investors determine the market value of a stock as compared to the company's earnings. In short, the P/E ratio shows what the market is willing to pay today for a stock based on its past or future earnings. A high P/E could mean that a stock's price is high relative to earnings and possibly overvalued. Conversely, a low P/E might indicate that the current stock price is low relative to earnings.

Data of the stock price and forecast EPS of Bank of America and JPMorgan as at end of the year 2021, obtained from NASDAQ site, and data on S&P 500 as obtained from WSJ website are presented below in the Table 5.3.

Table 5.3 Stock Price and EPS Forecast as at end of year 2021

Company / Index	Closing Price (US $)	EPS Forecast (US $)	P/E Forecast
Bank of America	44.49	3.5	
JPMorgan	158.35	14.97	
S&P 500	4605.38		22.82

Example 5.1

Calculate the P/E ratio for JPMorgan.

JPMorgan P/E ratio = 158.35 / 14.97 = 10.58.

In its absolute interpretation, without comparing to any other stock, it means that an investor is willing to pay almost US $11 for earning of US $1.

Example 5.2

Between JPMorgan and Bank of America which is overvalued?

Bank of America P/E ratio = 44.49 / 3.5 = 12.71

As P/E ratio of Bank of America is higher than that of JPMorgan, it means Bank of America stock is relatively overvalued.

Example 5.3

Compare P/E ratios of the two companies with that of S&P 500

P/E ratios of both are less than P/E ratio of S&P 500, indicating that both are undervalued compared to the index.

DuPont Model

From the shareholder perspective, which is the perspective of a stock market participant, RoE is very important. The ratio is obtained as

RoE = (Net Profit / Shareholder Equity) X 100

DuPont model decomposes RoE into three components, to gain insights into the three distinct aspects of the business. The three components of the DuPont model that makes up the RoE are:

$$RoE = \frac{Net\ Profit}{Net\ Sales} \times \frac{Net\ Sales}{Average\ Total\ Assets} \times \frac{Average\ Total\ Assets}{Share\ Holders'\ Equity} \times 100$$

Let us try to understand each one of the components.

- Net Profit Margin = Net Profits / Net Sales

This is the first part of the DuPont Model and it expresses the company's ability to generate profits. This is the PAT margin. A low net profit margin would indicate higher costs and increased competition

- Asset Turnover = Net Sales / Average Total assets

The second part of the model indicates how efficiently the company is using its assets to generate revenue. Higher ratio indicates that the company is using its assets efficiently. Low ratio indicates problems in management or production.

- Financial Leverage = Average Total Assets / Shareholders Equity

The third component, called the financial leverage helps to answer this question – For every unit of shareholders equity, how many units of assets does the company have? For example if the financial leverage is 4, it means that for every Rs.1 of equity, the company supports Rs.4 worth of assets. Higher financial leverage prompts investor caution.

The DuPont model breaks up the RoE formula into three distinct components, with each component giving an insight into the company's operating and financial capabilities

Qualitative Aspects

The fundamental analysis is mainly based on the quantitative aspects of the company. However, qualitative aspects can reveal what quantitative aspects do not. Some of the qualitative aspects the analysts look into are following:

- Management's background – Who are they? What is their background, experience, education? Do they have the merit to run the business? Are there any criminal cases against the promoters?

- Business ethics – Is the management involved in scams, bribery or unfair business practices?
- Corporate governance – Is there transparency in the appointment of directors, employee selection and compensation?
- Minority shareholders – How does the management treat minority shareholders? Do they consider their interest while taking corporate actions?
- Share transactions – Is the management buying/selling shares of the company through clandestine promoter groups?
- Related party transactions – Is the company tendering financial favours to known entities such as promoter's relatives, friends and vendors at the cost of the shareholders' funds?
- Salaries paid to promoters – Is the management paying themselves a hefty salary, usually a percentage of profits?
- Operator activity in stocks – Does the stock price display unusual price behaviour especially at a time when the promoter is transacting in the shares?
- Shareholders – Who are the significant shareholders in the firm? Who are the

people with above 1% of the outstanding shares of the company?
- Political affiliation – Is the company or its promoters too close to a political party? Does the business require constant political support?
- Promoter lifestyle – Are the promoters too flamboyant and loud about their lifestyle? Do they like to display their wealth?

Caveat

Efficient market hypothesis and random walk theory, which we will be discussing in the subsequent sections of this chapter, may give an impression that technical analysis and fundamental analysis theories do not help stock market participants. There is possibly an element of truth, though it is not fully correct. Portfolio managers and mutual funds continue to use both technical and fundamental analysis to build portfolios that give reasonably good return at acceptable levels of risk.

Individual investors, like you, can also derive benefit from these well accepted analyses. As authors of this book, we have a word of caution to you. Both technical and fundamental analysis are logical. Your negative emotions and traits should not sway you away from your rationality.

3. Bachelier and Random Walk Theory

*We are not subjected to a random walk of evolution,
nor are we subjected to a
deterministic script of Nature,
the truth lies somewhere in between –
we are part of teleological evolution*
— Alex M. Vikoulov

Louis Jean-Baptiste Alphonse Bachelier (1870 – 1946) was a French mathematician. He is credited with being the first person to model the stochastic process, called Brownian motion. His thesis, which discussed the use of Brownian motion to evaluate stock options, is historically the first paper to use advanced mathematics in the study of finance. Thus he is considered a pioneer in the study of financial mathematics and stochastic processes. It is interesting to note that Einstein used Brownian motion in 1905, five years after Bachelier did in 1900.

His PhD thesis *The Theory of Speculation*, was published in 1900. However, it took several decades for it to become integral part of further research in financial mathematics. The Figure 5.5 indicates the number of citations of the paper by further researchers over years:

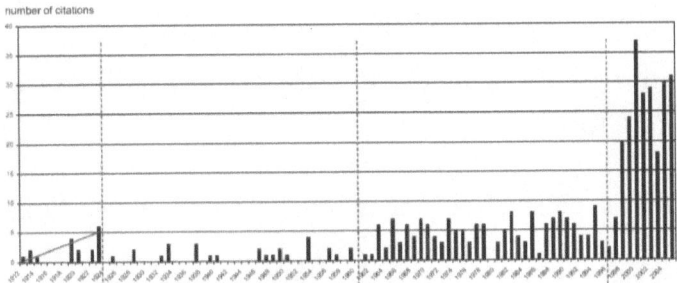

Figure 5.5 Number of Citations of Bachelier's Paper over Years

It can be seen from the Figure 5.5, that Bachelier's contribution was not recognized until 1964, when Cootner published a paper *The Random Character of Stock Market Prices*. Cootner not only made a reference to Bachelier's paper but also translated it into English.

In 1970, Fama developed Efficient Market Hypothesis from Random Walk character of stock prices proposed by Bachelier. In 1973, Black-Scholes used the concept extensively for their famous option pricing model.

Random Walk Theory (RWT) suggests that differences in stock prices have the same distribution and are independent of each other. Therefore, it assumes the past movement or trend of a stock price cannot be used to predict its future movement. In short, random walk theory proclaims that stocks take a random and unpredictable path that makes all methods of predicting stock prices futile in the long run.

RWT believes that it is impossible to outperform the market without assuming additional risk. It considers technical analysis undependable because chartists only buy or sell a security after an established trend has developed. Likewise, the theory finds fundamental analysis undependable due the poor quality of information collected and its susceptibility to be misinterpreted.

The most well-known practical example of RWT occurred in 1988 when the Wall Street Journal sought to test the theory by creating the annual Wall Street Journal Dartboard Contest, pitting professional investors against dart throwers for stock-picking supremacy.

After more than 140 contests, the experts won 87 contests and the dart throwers won 55. Further, the experts were able to beat the Dow Jones Industrial Average (DJIA) in only 76 contests. There are also stories about blindfolded monkeys outperforming the experts in stock selections!

However, critics of the theory contend that stocks do maintain price trends over time – in other words, that it is possible to outperform the market by carefully selecting entry and exit points for stock investments.

In Sum,

- RWT proposes that the changes in stock prices have the same distribution and are independent of each other
- It infers that the past movement or trend of a stock price or market cannot be used to predict its future movement
- It is impossible to outperform the market without assuming additional risk
- Technical analysis is undependable because it enables chartists in buying or selling a security after a move has occurred
- Fundamental analysis is undependable due to the often-poor quality of information collected that is prone to be misinterpreted
- RWT claims that investment advisors add little or no value to an investor's portfolio

4. Fama and Efficient Markets Hypothesis

Where is the wisdom we have lost in knowledge?
Where is the knowledge we have lost in information
— T.S. Eliot

The Random Walk Theory raised many eyebrows in 1973 when author Burton Malkiel used the term in his book, *A Random Walk Down Wall Street*. Unintentionally, the book popularized the Efficient Market Hypothesis (EMH).

The EMH states that stock prices fully reflect all available information and expectations. So current prices are the best approximation of the company's intrinsic value. This would preclude anyone from exploiting mispriced stocks consistently because price movements are mostly random and driven by unforeseen events.

A detailed analysis of efficient markets was presented by Eugene Fama in his seminal 1970 book, *Efficient Capital Markets: A Review of Theory and Empirical Work*. In his book he proposed the basic idea of EMH that it is virtually impossible to consistently beat the market as reflected by indices like S&P 500.

There are three forms of EMH depending on the type of information reflected in stock prices.

- Weak Efficiency - This form of EMH states that all past prices of a stock are reflected in today's stock price. Therefore, technical analysis cannot be used to predict and beat the market.
- Semi-Strong Efficiency - This form of EMH implies all public (but not non-public) information is reflected in a stock's current share price. Neither fundamental nor technical analysis can be used to achieve superior gains.
- Strong Efficiency – This is the purest form of EMH, which claims that all information in a market, whether public or private, is accounted for in a stock's price. This form of efficiency is very difficult to be achieved.

According to the EMH, stocks always trade at their fair value on exchanges, making it impossible for investors to purchase undervalued stocks or sell stocks for inflated prices. Therefore, it should be impossible to outperform the market through expert stock selection or market timing, and the only way an investor can obtain higher returns is by purchasing riskier investments.

Data compiled by Morningstar Inc., in its June 2019 Active/Passive Barometer study, supports the EMH. Morningstar compared active managers' returns in all categories against a composite made of related index funds and exchange-traded funds (ETFs). The study found that over a 10 year period beginning June 2009, only 23% of active managers were able to outperform their passive peers. While a percentage of active managers do outperform passive funds at some point, the challenge for investors is being able to identify which ones will do so over the long term.

Proponents of the EMH conclude that, because of the randomness of the market, investors could do better by investing in a low-cost, passive portfolio.

While academics point to a large body of evidence in support of EMH, an equal amount of dissension also exists. For example, investors such as Warren Buffett have consistently beaten the market over long periods, which is impossible according to the EMH. There are portfolio managers who have better track records compared to the others, and there are investment houses with more renowned research analysis than others.

EMH proponents, however, argue that those who outperform the market do so not out of skill but out of luck, due to the laws of probability. At any given time in a market with a large number of players, some will outperform the mean, while others will underperform.

Detractors of the EMH also point to events such as the 1987 stock market crash, when the Dow Jones Industrial Average (DJIA) fell by over 20 percent in a single day, and asset bubbles as evidence that stock prices can seriously deviate from their fair values.

There are certainly some markets that are less efficient than others. An inefficient market is one in which an asset's price does not accurately reflect its true value. Market inefficiencies may exist due to information asymmetries, low liquidity and high transaction costs. We feel that market psychology and human emotion as more important reasons. The more the rational participants are engaged in a market, the more efficient it should become.

In Sum,

- EMH states that share prices reflect all information.

- Based on the information under consideration, there are three forms of EMH – Weak, Semi-Strong and Strong.
- EMH hypothesizes that stocks trade at their fair market value on exchanges.
- Theoretically, neither technical nor fundamental analysis can produce risk-adjusted excess returns consistently.
- Proponents of EMH posit that investors benefit from investing in a low-cost, passive portfolio.
- Opponents of EMH believe that it is possible to beat the market and that stocks can deviate from their fair market values.

5. Sharpe and the Capital Asset Pricing Model

It is not a calculated risk if you haven't calculated it
— Naved Abdali

Let us recollect the Example 4.46 on investing in a café or an ice cream parlour in a hill station in the coming summer. In order to minimize the risk due to vagaries of rainfall, you decided to invest in both the café and parlour.

Similarly you build a portfolio by selecting stocks whose returns move in opposite directions. You can select negatively correlated stocks by using correlation coefficient and diversify your portfolio.

No matter how much you diversify your portfolio, some level of risk will always exist. So investors naturally seek a rate of return that compensates for that risk. The Capital Asset Pricing Model (CAPM) helps to calculate the portfolio risk and what return an investor should expect on the portfolio.

The CAPM was developed by the financial economist William Sharpe, set out in his 1970 book, *Portfolio Theory and Capital Markets*. His model starts with the idea that any investment contains two types of risk:

- Systematic Risk – The risk is inherent in market and cannot be diversified away. Interest rates, recessions, and wars are examples of systematic risks.
- Unsystematic Risk – The risk is specific to individual stocks. It represents the component of a stock's return that is not correlated with general market moves.

Modern portfolio theory shows that unsystematic risk, specific to a stock can be removed or at least mitigated through building a diversified portfolio. The trouble is that diversification does not solve the problem of systematic risk; even a portfolio holding all the shares in the stock market can't eliminate that risk. Therefore, when calculating a deserved return, investors need to factor systematic risk.

CAPM has evolved as a way to measure the systematic risk. Sharpe found that the return on an individual stock, or a portfolio, should equal its cost of capital. The CAPM formula describes the relationship between risk and expected return.

CAPM's starting point is the risk-free rate R_f, typically a 10-year government bond yield. A premium, one that equity investors expect as compensation for the extra risk they take, is to be added to R_f. This equity market premium is the expected return from the market R_m less the risk-free rate of return R_f multiplied by a factor, called β (Beta). β is the regression coefficient of stock return on market return, with which we are already familiar. Thus CAPM formula is -

$$R = R_f + \beta \times (R_m - R_f)$$

As per CAPM, a riskier investment should earn a premium over the risk-free rate. The amount over the risk-free rate is obtained by the equity market premium multiplied by its Beta.

Example 5.4

If the stock's Beta is 2.0, the risk-free rate is 3%, and the market rate of return is 7%, find the expected return of the stock.

Expected return of the stock R = 3 + 2 X (7 -3) = 11%

According to CAPM, Beta is the only relevant measure of a stock's risk. It measures a stock's relative volatility, that is, it shows how much the price of a particular stock goes up or down compared with how much the market goes up or down. It is obtained by calculating regression coefficient between stock and market returns.

If a share price moves exactly in line with the market, then the stock's Beta is 1. A stock with a Beta of 1.5 would rise by 15% if the market rises by 10% and fall by 15% if the market falls by 10%.

The model presents a simple theory. The theory says that the only reason an investor should earn more, on an average, by investing in one stock rather than another is that one stock is riskier. Not surprisingly, the model has come to dominate modern financial theory.

But it is not entirely clear whether the model works or not. The big sticking point is Beta. When Eugene Fama and Kenneth French looked at the share returns on the New York Stock Exchange, the American Stock Exchange, and Nasdaq, they found that differences in Betas over a lengthy period did not explain the performance of different stocks. The findings seem to suggest that CAPM may not work always.

In Sum,

- Diversification helps in reducing specific risk of stocks

- Diversification can be achieved by including uncorrelated stocks in the portfolio
- Diversification cannot remove systematic risk
- A relevant measure of stock's risk is Beta
- Beta is obtained as regression coefficient
- Beta provides a useful measure that helps investors determine what return they can expect on an investment, in exchange for putting their money at risk on it
- The CAPM may not be a perfect theory but the spirit of CAPM is correct

6. Ross and Arbitrage Pricing Theory

> *The record of professionals does not suggest that sufficient predictability exists in the stock market to produce exploitable arbitrage opportunities*
> — Burton G. Malkiel

Arbitrage pricing theory (APT) is an alternative to the Capital Asset Pricing Model (CAPM) for explaining returns on assets or portfolios. It was developed by the economist Stephen Ross in the 1970s. Over the years, APT has grown in popularity for its relatively simpler assumptions. However, APT is a lot more difficult to apply in practice because it requires considerable amount of data and complex statistical analysis.

APT is a multi-factor technical model based on the relationship between a financial asset's expected return and its risk. The model is designed to capture the sensitivity of the asset's returns to changes in certain macroeconomic variables.

APT is based on the following assumptions:

- Asset returns are explained by systematic factors

- Investors can build a portfolio of assets where specific risk is eliminated through diversification
- No arbitrage opportunity exists among well-diversified portfolios
- If any arbitrage opportunities do exist, they will be exploited away by investors

According to the research of Stephen Ross and Richard Roll, the most important factors are the following:

- Production
- Inflation
- Shifts in risk premiums
- Changes in Treasury Bond Yields

According to them, if no surprise happens in the change of the above factors, the actual return will be equal to the expected return. However, in case of unanticipated changes to the factors, the actual return will depend on factor sensitivities.

Recall that in the CAPM, we derived the Beta, which measures asset sensitivity to market return, by simply regressing actual asset returns against market returns. Deriving the factors' Beta in the case of APT is pretty much similar.

For the purpose of illustrating the technique of estimating sensitivity let us take the S&P 500 Total Return Index and the NASDAQ Composite Total Return Index as proxies for well-diversified portfolios. For simplicity, we'll assume that we know the risk-free return is 2%. We'll also assume that the annual expected return of the portfolios are 7% for the S&P 500 Total Return Index and 9% for the NASDAQ Composite Total Return Index.

We have to determine the systematic factors by which portfolio returns are explained. Let us assume that the real gross domestic product (GDP) growth rate and the 10-year Treasury bond yield change are the factors that we need.

We can run a regression on historical quarterly data of each index against quarterly real GDP growth rates and quarterly T-bond yield changes. The regression coefficients are the Betas for GDP Growth Rate and T-Bond Yield Change. For hypothetical data, the Betas may look like the results in the Table 5.4.

Table 5.4 Betas for APT Illustration

	GDP Growth Rate	T-Bond Yield Change
S&P 500 Total Return Index	3.5	0.05
NASDAQ Composite Total Return Index	4.5	0.1

Note that both portfolios have -

- quite high sensitivity to GDP growth rates
- very low sensitivity to T-bond yield change

Self-Assessment

Reflect for a moment whether these Betas are consistent with our intuition.

In Sum,

- Arbitrage is the practice of simultaneously buying and selling the same item at two different prices for a risk-free profit.
- APT assumes that market inefficiencies arise from time to time but are kept in check through the work of arbitrageurs who identify and immediately eliminate such opportunities as they arise.
- APT is formalized using a multi-factor formula that relates the linear relationship

between an asset's expected return and various macroeconomic variables.
- The drawback of arbitrage pricing theory is that it does not specify the systematic factors, but leaves it to analysts to find them by regressing historical portfolio returns against factors such as real GDP growth rates, inflation changes, term structure changes, risk premium changes, and so on.
- Regression equations make it possible to assess which systematic factors explain portfolio returns and which do not.

7. Keynes and Animal Spirits

Most of our decisions to do something positive, can only be taken as the result of animal spirits— a spontaneous urge to action rather than inaction, and not as the outcome of a weighted average of quantitative benefits multiplied by quantitative probabilities
— John Maynard Keynes

The famous British economist, John Maynard Keynes, used the term animal spirits to describe how people arrive at financial decisions, including buying and selling of securities, in the times of economic stress or uncertainty. In Keynes's 1936 publication, *The General Theory of Employment, Interest, and Money*, he speaks of animal spirits as the human emotions that affect consumer confidence.

Today, animal spirits describe the psychological and emotional factors that drive investors to take action when faced with high levels of volatility in the stock markets. Animal spirits represent the emotions of confidence, hope, fear, and pessimism that can affect financial decision-making, which in turn can fuel or hamper economic growth. If spirits are low, then confidence levels will be low, which will drive down a promising economy even if the fundamentals are strong. Likewise, if spirits are high, confidence among participants in the economy will be high, and market prices will soar.

According to the theory of animal spirits, the decisions of business leaders are based on intuition and the behaviour of their competitors rather than on solid analysis. Keynes understood that in times of economic upheaval, irrational thoughts might influence people as they pursue their financial self-interests.

Keynes further posited in *The General Theory* that trying to estimate the future yield of various industries, companies, or activities using general knowledge and available insight amounts to very little and sometimes to nothing. He proposed that the only way people can take decisions in an uncertain environment is if animal spirits guide them.

Animal spirits often manifest as market psychology defined by either fear or greed. The term irrational exuberance has been used to describe investor enthusiasm that drives asset prices far higher than what fundamentals can justify. Simply tagging dot-com to the name of a company during the period 1995 to 2000 increased its market value to extraordinary levels, with start-ups showing zero earnings, commanding very high share prices. The crash that followed saw the Nasdaq index tumble. By the end of 2001, most dot-com stocks had gone burst.

Another example was the lead-up to the 2008-09 financial crisis and the Great Recession, when the markets were rife with financial innovations. Creative use of both new and existing financial products like collateralized debt obligations (CDOs) abounded, particularly in the housing market. Initially, this trend was thought to be positive, that is until the new financial instruments were found to be deceptive. At this point, investor confidence plummeted, a sell-off ensued, and the markets plunged. A clear case of animal spirits run amok.

In 2009, two economists, George A. Akerlof and Robert J. Shiller published their book, *Animal Spirits: How Human Psychology Drives the Economy, and Why it Matters for Global Capitalism*. The authors argue that although animal spirits are important, it is equally important that the government actively intervenes to control them via economic policymaking when necessary. Otherwise, the authors postulate, the spirits might follow their own devices and result in the kind of overindulgence that we saw in the 2008 financial crisis.

Animal spirits refer to the tendency for investment prices to rise and fall based on human emotions rather than intrinsic value. This theory, however, has been critiqued by some economists who argue that markets are nonetheless efficient and that individual irrationality washes out in the aggregate. Other critics argue that bubbles are not the result of mass psychology, but are due to large increases in the money supply. The argument often stems from Austrian economic theory or libertarianism.

In some ways, Keynes' insights into human behaviour was the forerunner to the development of behavioural economics decades later. His animal spirits thesis threw a monkey wrench into the assumptions of efficiency and rationality in markets.

In Sum,

- The British economist, John Maynard Keynes used the term animal spirits for the first time in 1936 in the context of stock markets.

- Animal spirits refer to the ways that human emotion can drive financial decision-making in uncertain environments and volatile times.
- Animal spirits essentially account for market psychology and in particular the role of emotion and herd mentality in investing.
- We may observe the concept of animal spirits in action during financial crises, including the Great Recession of 2007–2009.
- Animal spirits are used to help explain why people behave irrationally, and are the forerunner to modern behavioural economics.

8. Nobel Laureates and Behavioural Economics

Most human beings are irrational most of the time & hence they have weird perceptions
— Dharmendra Rai

a) Herbert Simon and Bounded Rationality

Herbert Alexander Simon was an economist, political scientist and cognitive psychologist, whose primary research interest was decision-making within organizations. He is best known for the theories of *bounded rationality*. His research was noted for its interdisciplinary nature and spanned across the fields of cognitive science, computer science, public administration, management, and political science. He received the Nobel Memorial Prize in Economic Sciences in 1978.

Bounded rationality is the idea that we make decisions that are rational, but within the limits of the information and time available to us to make that decision. It also argues that we have limited mental capabilities to make decisions so the rationality to human decisions is limited.

Decision-makers usually simplify the decision-making process into a couple of key factors. They may be price, value, or something else, but the key factor is that a decision is made that satisfies the basic criteria.

Example 5.5

You are at the store to select a dessert for your husband and two children. You have three options, a chocolate cake, a blueberry cheesecake, or cookies. Your husband's favourite is chocolate cake, whilst your first child, Jessica, prefers the cheesecake, and Charlotte prefers cookies. Cookies are the cheapest and can be saved for the next few days. Chocolate cake can also be saved for the next day. There are so many such factors to consider to reach an optimal decision. Rather than spend half an hour deliberating, you just choose the cheapest, simply based on cost.

b) Gary Becker and Motives and Consumer Mistakes

Gary Stanley Becker was a professor of economics and sociology. He is also considered the leader of the third generation of the Chicago school of economics with a revolutionary price theory. He received the 1992 Nobel Memorial Prize in Economic Sciences for *having extended the domain of economic theory to aspects of human behaviour which had previously been dealt with—if at all—by other social science disciplines such as sociology, demography and criminology.*

He argued that many different types of human behaviour can be seen as rational and utility maximizing. His approach included altruistic behaviour of humans by defining individuals' utility appropriately.

Example 5.6

There are a series of shops on a road selling shoes. The choice of the shop can be based on quality, price or service. However, it can as well be based on the appearance of the shop. The motive is purely emotional.

Example 5.7

When you visited a friend's house, you noticed a chandelier that looked extremely attractive. You check with the friend the shop and price. Your husband alerts you that that particular chandelier does not suit your house design and décor. However, you go and buy it immediately. The purchase decision is based on imitation motive.

Example 5.8

You are ordering online a set of batteries. As you are about to order the batteries, there is a suggestion to buy attractive toys along with the batteries. You include a toy in your shopping cart. Your purchase it not based on your need but on an impulse.

c) Daniel Kahneman and Amos Tversky and Prospect Theory

Daniel Kahneman is a psychologist and economist notable for his work on the psychology of judgment and decision-making, as well as behavioural economics, for which he was awarded the 2002 Nobel Memorial Prize in Economic Sciences (shared with Vernon L. Smith). His empirical findings challenge the assumption of human rationality prevailing in modern economic theory.

Amos Nathan Tversky was a mathematical psychologist, a student of cognitive science and a figure in the discovery of systematic human cognitive bias and handling of risk.

Prospect theory, proposed by Kahneman and Tversky, assumes that losses and gains are valued differently, and thus individuals make decisions based on perceived gains instead of perceived losses. Also known as the *loss-aversion theory*, the general concept is that if two choices are put before an individual, both equal, with one presented in terms of potential gains and the other in terms of possible losses, the former option will be chosen. The concept is illustrated through examples 5.9 and 5.10.

Example 5.9

Consider two options. In the first, you can straightaway take US $50. In the second, you can flip a coin and win US $100 if you call it right, or nothing if your call is wrong.

Under such a scenario of certainty of gain, you opt for the guaranteed option.

Example 5.10

Consider two options. In the first, you have to straightaway give US $50. In the second, you can flip a coin, lose nothing if you call it right, or lose US $100 if you call it wrong.

Under such a scenario of certainty of loss, you choose the chance option.

Example 5.11

A study in 1995 by the American Psychological Association at the 1992 Barcelona Olympics found that bronze medallists were significantly happier following the results than those who won a silver medal. So why were bronze medallists happier?

The behaviour is explained by counterfactual thinking. Simply put, the silver medallist was expecting and aiming for gold, and was, therefore, disappointed to not have met that aim. However, the bronze medallist did not expect to be on the podium, so a bronze medal exceeded expectations.

d) Richard Thaler and Nudge Theory

Richard H. Thaler is an economist and Professor of Behavioural Science and Economics. He won the 2017 Nobel Memorial Prize in Economic Sciences for *incorporating psychologically realistic assumptions into analyses of economic decision-making*. By exploring the consequences of limited rationality, social preferences, and lack of self-control, he has shown how these human traits systematically affect individual decisions as well as market outcomes.

Nudge is a concept in behavioural science, political theory and behavioural economics which proposes positive reinforcement and indirect suggestions as ways to influence the behaviour and decision making of groups or individuals.

The nudge theory is gaining traction in the public policy space with governments or organizations increasingly using this 'non-regulatory' tool to achieve desired objectives, as evidenced in immunizations, organ donation and tax compliances. For instance, organ donations are observed to have gone up, when the consent was made as a default option compared to when people were required to give an explicit consent. Better dietary discipline was also observed in staff canteens by positioning healthy food to catch the attention of the staff. The nudge strategy works by convincing staff that they are doing it all by their choice.

Example 5.12

When you buy a burger, you are likely to purchase fries and soft drinks when they're offered as a suggestion.

Example 5.13

When there is an additional cost for plastic bags at stores, you are less likely to purchase them, thereby reducing plastic consumption.

Example 5.14

Schools often hang posters or pictures of inspirational leaders and their quotes to encourage students to think in a particular way.

Self-Test 5.1

You have been asking your 10-year-old daughter to tidy up her room for the past few days. She finds some excuse to avoid this responsibility every time. What do you do –

a) Warn her that you would punish her
b) Bribe her with a chocolate
c) Suggest a game to her – who can organize things the fastest
d) Leave her out of you frustration

Greater Fool Theory

Let us end this chapter with a theory, which is strictly not a theory, but is behind several irrational decisions and transactions. If you believe that there is always a greater fool willing to pay a higher price, you can buy any stock at any given price. It is anybody's guess what drives you to believe that there is a greater fool waiting to hand over handsome profits to you!

CHAPTER VI

Historical Market Events

Abstract

Tulip Mania is possibly the first recorded asset bubble burst. Since then, there have been such bubbles and bursts in the history of markets, the most recent being the global financial crisis. All the bubbles go through phases from excitement, entry, euphoria and edginess to exit. Emotional traits like greed and fear have always been behind growth and burst of bubbles. Interestingly, the emotions continue to play dominant role despite several such historical events.

Keywords

Asset Bubbles, Bubble Bursts, Euphoria, Greed, Fear, Tulip Mania, Vienna Stock Exchange Crash, Wall Street Crash, Black Monday, Dot-Com Burst, Global Financial Crisis

1. 5Es of Asset Bubble Life Cycle

*A pin lies in wait for every bubble.
And when the two eventually meet,
a new wave of investors learns some very old lessons*
- Warren Buffet

It is difficult to define a financial asset bubble but there is a basic characteristic behind each bubble. Most participants suspend their rationality when the speculative price surge is occurring to recognize later that it is an unwarranted euphoria.

It is unfortunate that by the time the realization dawns on participants, it is too late. On one hand the individuals themselves end up with financial losses. On the other, which is more dangerous, the economic sectors go into deep trouble, leading to significant cost of recovery to countries.

We identify five phases in a bubble, which we call 5Es. They are Excitement, Entry, Euphoria, Edginess and Exit, though it is possible that some of these phases may overlap. The first three are bubble growth phases and the last two are bubble burst phases.

- **Excitement**

There is an excitement when investors get enamoured by a new paradigm, such as an innovative new technology like dot-coms during 1997 to 2000 or historically low interest rates like federal funds rates during July 2000 to June 2003.

- **Entry**

Following excitement, prices rise slowly at first but then gain momentum as more and more participants enter the market, setting the stage for the next phase of euphoria. During the entry phase, the asset attracts widespread attention. Fear of missing out on what could be once-in-a-lifetime opportunity draws an increasing number of participants into the fold.

- **Euphoria**

During this phase, caution is thrown to the wind, as asset prices skyrocket. Valuations reach extreme levels and new valuation measures and metrics are touted to justify the relentless rise. The greater fool theory plays out everywhere.

- **Edginess**

In this phase, warning signs that the bubble would burst soon appear. A few smart people heed to the warnings and start taking profits by selling. But estimating the exact time of the bubble burst is difficult. Many will be waiting for the right time.

- **Exit**

When many are edgy to sell, it only takes a relatively minor event to prick the bubble. In the panic stage, everyone just wants to exit at any price. With supply surpassing demand, asset prices slide further. Asset prices reverse course and descend very rapidly, faster than their ascent. Once the bubble is pricked, it cannot inflate again.

Theoretically, there are infinite categories of asset bubbles. After all, a speculative frenzy can arise over anything, from cryptocurrencies like Bitcoin to meme stocks like Gamestop to housing prices to tulip bulbs. But in general, asset bubbles can be broken down into four broad categories:

- **Stock Market Bubbles**
  Involve stocks that rise rapidly in price, often out of proportion to their companies' fundamental value. These bubbles can include the overall stock market, exchange-traded funds (ETFs), or equities.

- **Asset Market Bubbles**
  Involve industries, sections or sectors of the economy, other than the stock market. Real estate is a classic example. Currencies like the US dollar or Euro also fall into this category.
- **Credit Market Bubbles**
  Involve a sudden surge in consumer or business loans, debt instruments, and other forms of credit. Specific examples of assets include corporate bonds or government bonds, student loans and mortgages.
- **Commodity Market Bubbles**
  Involve an increase in the price of traded commodities such as gold, oil, industrial metals, or agricultural crops.

Negative emotional traits which we discussed in Chapter II, play an important role in various phases of the bubble. Especially greed and fear – greed during the first three bubble growth phases and fear during the last two bubble burst phases.

Self-Assessment

We, in this chapter, will be presenting the following six historical events that went through the asset bubble life cycle:

1. Tulip Mania (1634)
2. Vienna Stock Exchange Crash (1873)
3. Wall Street Crash (1929)
4. Black Monday (1987)
5. Dot-Com Burst (2000)
6. Global Financial Crisis (2008)

After reading each event, write down what would have been your action in each phase. Also identify the emotional traits responsible for your action.

You can use the format in the Table 6.1 for each of the six events.

Table 6.1 Phase-wise Action and Trait

Phase	Action	Trait
Excitement		
Entry		
Euphoria		
Edginess		
Exit		
Would you have gained or lost during the event?		
If so, which trait is responsible for your gain or loss?		

2. Tulip Mania (1634)

> *Tulips were a tray of jewels*
> — E.M. Forster

Who would have imagined that a bulb of a flower could cost as much as a mansion on the banks of Amsterdam Grand Canal? The much talked about Tulip Mania of 1634 goes on to prove that nothing is unworthy of creating a bubble. All that is required is a group of people, majority of them, believing in the value of anything.

Tulips were flowers known for their bold colours and beautiful shape, before they were ignominiously linked to the financial crisis. They were imported from Turkey to Europe in late 1500s. Given their exotic looks and fragile nature, they soon became a status symbol to be owned by the affluent and later became a commodity that everybody yearned to possess, not necessarily for their beauty or intrinsic worth, but for their perceived value.

A bit of game theory would help understand the situation better. The value of tulip is not determined by how much the holders thinks it is, but how much the prospective buyers think it is, who in turn, would think how much their prospective counterpart would value the tulip and so on. As long as the chain of imaginary counterparts continues, the price of tulip can technically go up infinitely. As tulips need time to be planted and grown, there was always a production lag and the supply could not match the galloping demand, leading to sky rocketing of prices.

By 1636, tulips were being traded in stock exchanges in the Netherlands. People took leveraged bets by using margined derivatives to buy tulips. At the peak of the tulip mania, it was estimated that the best of tulips were costing about an unimaginable US $750,000 as per 2022 prices.

Subsequently, the prices of tulips started to correct. As many participants bought tulips on borrowed money, there was a scramble to exit which caused further precipitous fall in prices forcing more participants to exit. By the time the tide of exuberance receded and the prices returned to normalcy in 1638, there were many participants who were left poorer and probably wiser.

There are many narratives of the Tulip Mania ranging from those that describe vividly the catastrophic impact it had on the wealth of the country and the fate of people, to those that see the incident as a mere exaggeration created to etch into public discourse the ills of excessive greed and the lesson that whatever goes up must come down. A lesson that is so obvious that people often ignore. The scientific formulation of laws of gravity, however, came half a century later.

Were the people so irrational to have believed that the prices could only go up and that the passion for tulips would last forever? In hindsight, definitely yes. But it was perfectly rational for people to buy goods whose prices are expected to go up and sell when the prices are expected to fall. However, when the same thing is done on a large scale fuelled by leverage, it leads to creation of bubbles and crashes that follow. It was also perfectly rational for farmers to produce more tulips sensing the demand, but when the same is done by everyone, the supply outstripped demand leading to crash in prices.

Tulip mania remains more of a parable of greed and excesses accentuated by herd mentality. A parable whose lessons the world never seriously learnt.

3. Vienna Stock Exchange Crash (1873)

> *Wisdom, itself, is often an abstraction associated not with fact or reality but with the man who asserts it and the manner of its assertion*
> — John Kenneth Galbraith

Equity markets and manias appear to be having some inexplicable links, inasmuch as these markets seem to provide suitable avenues for the exuberance and irrationality to manifest. The Vienna stock exchange crash of 1873 would go down in the history as one of such episodes causing a very long depression and devastating impact on the continents on either side of the Atlantic.

There are multitude of factors that led to the legendary crash resulting in closing down of stock exchanges, suspension of deposit conversions by banks and the associated humungous productivity losses. While there are many arguments as to the likely causes of the crash, most narratives begin with the post-war exuberance in both the United States and the Europe.

Franco-Prussian war immunities paid by France to Germany led to huge speculative bubble in the newly unified Germany, which extended to Austria. The 'miracle harvest' of 1867 in Austria witnessed establishment of more than 1,000 joint stock companies. The uncontrolled speculation on the stock exchange of Vienna eventually witnessed a massive fall on a Black Friday (May 9, 1873) on the back of panic selling. The crash had impacted the Vienna World Exhibition organized during the period, leading to an immediate fall in number of visitors and an eventual contraction of economy and erosion of wealth in Europe.

As the boom was building in Europe, the US too was witnessing a post-civil war economic expansion, fuelled by the massive expansion of railway network. The boom was being funded by European lenders. The subsequent developments in Europe cast a long shadow on such funding, with the European lenders reducing their risk appetite leading to drying up of the European investment. The demonetization of silver by Germany also forced the United States to move to a de facto Gold Standard which led to currency shortage. All these events had a devastating impact on the US financial markets.

The sudden bust of railroad boom saw demise of many financial firms which had overextended themselves. Jay Cooke & Company, one of the most notable US institutions, which had marketed US $500 million of bonds issued by the Union during the Civil war, had to be closed on the back of the failure of the Northern Pacific Railroad. Events unfolded quickly with more firms failing and the contagion spreading to banks and stock exchanges. The stock markets crashed by 11.2 per cent on Sep 20, 1873 and the exchange had to be closed only to be opened after 10 days.

Massive bank runs forced banks to suspend convertibility of deposits fuelling further panic. The 'Great Panic' as it is notoriously referred to, left an indelible impression on public memory and unforgettable scar on economies and people's lives. The event which was initially called the 'Great Depression' owing to its magnitude, was later called the 'Long Depression' referring to its prolonged impact.

While there are many narratives to explain the causes of this panic, the primary theme is the exuberance which became unsustainable. As history often teaches, it becomes very difficult to remain rational, when good times are building up, but that is precisely the time, the inner voice of rationality and reason needs to be heeded to.

4. Wall Street Crash (1929)

> *I will tell you the secret to getting rich on Wall Street.*
> *You try to be greedy when others are fearful.*
> *And you try to be fearful when others are greedy*
> — Warren Buffett

Of all the crises that preceded it and most that followed, the episode of stock market crash is rightly called 'Great', as the devastation and the consequent lessons left behind by the Great Crash of 1929 and the Great Depression that followed, were significant.

The post war optimism of the Roaring Twenties, fueled by massive investments into American industrial sector and steep increase in consumer spending on the back of migration of rural Americans to cities, quickly led to exuberance resulting in huge inflows into stock markets. The stock market indices witnessed a six-fold increase in the 9-year run preceding the 1929 crash. Funds found their way into stock markets with home owners mortgaging their houses and liquidating their deposits, eagerly wanting to be a part of the American Dream. Margin financing helped investors in taking huge bets even with small amounts of their own funds.

As we have been seeing in every crisis, it was extremely difficult to discern the growth from speculation. Many common investors, blinded by the curse of 'information asymmetry', adopted the easier option of following the crowd and joining the bandwagon. Intermittent warning by the Fed did not find much traction with the eager investors. So much was the faith in the fundamentals of the stock market that the legendary Irving Fisher was quoted to have concluded that *'stock prices have reached what looks like a permanently high plateau'*.

Like all things, whether good or bad, coming to an end, even this long, but unsustainable run came to an eventual end. Rate actions by Fed to arrest the speculation, *inter alia*, other factors such as crash of London Stock Exchange in September 1929, etc. led to huge sell-off of stocks on the fateful Black Thursday on October 24, 1929, followed by Black Monday and Black Tuesday; October 28 and 29 crashes are the worst two-day decline in history thus far! The corrections continued till 1932 when Dow recorded the lowest level in 20th Century. Such was the fall that the indices did not return to their earlier levels of September 1929 for the next 25 years!

The post mortem of the crisis unraveled many a great lesson for the policy makers, central banks and regulators. Investment banking was separated from commercial banking through the famous, now repealed Glass-Steagall Act, 1933, indicating that we do not learn from our mistakes. Central Bankers learnt that it would not only be difficult to identify an asset bubble in the making, but also futile and counterproductive to bust it by their policy actions, a lesson that was later called into question during the Global Financial Crisis of 2008. Like many other crises, the Great Crash also left people poor and economies crippled for many years. Ironically, it took another World War to bring back the American Economy back on track with massive war time investments triggering the economy.

Notwithstanding the many sophisticated causes and lessons that the Great Crash unearthed, the episode does have the two most common and powerful enemies – greed and fear, greed for easy and quick money and the fear of missing out on opportunities of both buying and selling.

5. Black Monday (1987)

> *Sometimes it seems as though each new step towards AI, rather than producing something which everyone agrees is real intelligence, merely reveals what real intelligence is not*
> — Douglas Hofstadter

Black Monday occurred on October 19, 1987, when the Dow Jones Industrial Average (DJIA) lost almost 22% in a single day. The event marked the beginning of a global stock market decline, and Black Monday became one of the most notorious days in financial history. By the end of the month, most of the major exchanges had dropped more than 20%.

The cause of the massive stock market drop could not be attributed to any single cause. Several events coalesced to create an atmosphere of panic among investors. For example, the trade deficit of the United States widened with respect to other countries. Crises, such as a standoff between Kuwait and Iran, which threatened to disrupt oil supplies, also made investors jittery. The role of media as an amplifying factor for these developments has also come in for criticism. While there are many theories that attempt to explain why the crash occurred, most agree that mass panic caused the crash to escalate. Economists have attributed the crash to a combination of all such events and the advent of automated trading systems.

Though not as dominant force as they are today, automated trading systems were increasingly making their presence felt at several Wall Street firms. They played an important role in the increased market volatility. In automated trading, human decision-making is taken out of the equation, and buy or sell orders are generated automatically based on the price levels of benchmark indexes or specific stocks.

The models used at that time were relatively new and tended to produce strong positive feedback, generating more buy orders when prices were rising and more sell orders when prices began to fall. It appears that the systems mimicked human behavioural trends of greed and fear. We will discuss details of automated trading systems in Chapter VII.

Since Black Monday, a number of protective mechanisms have been built into the market to prevent panic selling, such as trading curbs and circuit breakers. However, high-frequency trading (HFT) algorithms driven by supercomputers move massive volume in just milliseconds, which still increase volatility.

6. Dot-Com Burst (2000)

> *Quality sells itself - No hype needed*
> — Brandi L. Bates

Bckground

The 1993 release of Mosaic and subsequent web browsers gave computer users access to the World Wide Web, popularizing use of the Internet. With the multiple uses of the internet, the number of internet users increased. It led to advances in computing and connectivity and to what was fashionably called dot-com companies.

Dot-com

Many investors were eager to invest in any company with the prefix dot-com in its name. Venture capital was easy to raise. Investment banks, which profited significantly from initial public offerings (IPO), fuelled speculation and encouraged investment in technology. A combination of

- the rapidly increasing stock prices in the quaternary sector of the economy
- confidence that the companies would turn future profits

created an environment in which many investors were willing to overlook traditional metrics, such as P/E ratios. The overall exuberance on technological advancements led to a stock market bubble. Between 1995 and 2000, the Nasdaq Composite stock market index rose 400%.

An unprecedented amount of personal investing occurred during the boom and stories of people quitting their jobs to trade on the financial market were common. At the height of the boom, it was possible for a promising dot-com company to become a public company via an IPO and raise a substantial amount of money even if it had never made a profit or in some cases had not realized any material revenue. People who received employee stock options became instant paper millionaires.

Burst

Around the turn of the millennium, spending on technology was volatile as companies were preparing for the Y2K. There were concerns that computer systems would have trouble changing their clock and calendar systems from 1999 to 2000 which might trigger wider social or economic problems.

On March 20, 2000, *Barron's* featured a cover article, *Burning Up; Warning: Internet companies are running out of cash*, which predicted the imminent bankruptcy of many Internet companies. This led many people to rethink their investments.

On Friday, April 14, 2000, the Nasdaq Composite index fell 9%, ending a week in which it fell 25%. Investors were forced to sell stocks ahead of Tax Day, the due date to pay taxes on gains realized in the previous year.

By June 2000, dot-com companies were forced to re-evaluate their spending on advertising campaigns.

By the end of the stock market downturn of 2002, stocks had lost US $5 trillion in market capitalization since the peak. At its trough on October 9, 2002, the NASDAQ-100 had dropped to 1,114, down 78% from its peak.

A classic case of speculative euphoria on technology! A mad rush not to miss the bus!!

7. Global Financial Crisis (2008)

The surest way to ruin a man who doesn't know how to handle money is to give him some
— George Bernard Shaw

A very recent event is the global financial crisis that devastated most of the countries in the world for a fairly long period. The origin can be traced to the 9/11 terrorist attack that led to recession in USA. The Fed started lowering its funds rate.

Interest rates on adjustable-rate mortgages, which were based on the Fed funds rate, became cheaper. Many homeowners who couldn't afford conventional mortgages were delighted to get these easy loans. Most of the US citizens who could potentially take a mortgage took it.

During this period, various financial innovative products emerged. The products were so designed to give profits to several market players. The system worked roughly as below:

- Commercial banks securitized mortgages and created mortgage backed securities (MBS)

- Investment banks borrowed millions or even billions to buy MBS from commercial banks
- Investment banks packaged MBS to create collaterized debt obligation (CDO)
- Hedge funds borrowed to buy CDOs from Investment banks
- Hedge funds sold CDOs to investors
- Insurance companies sold insurance to investors to mitigate risk relating to CDOs

It was basically risk-free for the bank and the hedge fund. The investors took all the risk of default, but they didn't worry about the risk because they had insurance sold by insurance companies. Thanks to the insurance, investors snapped up the CDOs. In time, everyone owned them, including pension funds, large banks, hedge funds, and even individual investors.

Many of the home loan borrowers with adjustable-rate loans didn't realize the rates would be reset. In 2004, the Fed started raising rates. Homeowners were hit with payments they couldn't afford. They started defaulting.

In order to ensure that the market players continue to benefit from innovative products like MBS and

CDO, the banks started lending money to insolvent home loan borrowers to take out a new mortgage. The borrowers did not see a problem as they were able to own a second house as an investment.

However, defaults increased and there were more houses for sale. As the supply exceeded demand, the prices started falling sharply. Real estate prices crashed. Home loan borrowers were not willing to repay more than the value of the house. The credit market suffered. CDOs whose value is derived from the value of underlying mortgages became worthless. Insurance companies were also in trouble.

The housing market bubble burst led to banking crisis in 2007, which spread to Wall Street in 2008. All the players - Homeowners, Banks, Hedge Funds, Investors and Insurance Companies - did not want to lose an opportunity to make high profits. They all had their own reasons to believe that the bubble would never burst! The world suffered due to their irrational exuberance as crisis spread to real estate, credit and stock markets and engulfed almost all countries on the globe.

8. Crypto Growth

Any Physical or Digital Commodity that is traded is subject to bubble and crash
— Gun Gun Febrianza

Self-Test 6.1

Write a story about crypto growth during 2017-22 and your assessment of its future. Do you think a crypto bubble burst is likely?

Self-Assessment

Collate all self-assessments you made after each of the six historical events as per the format in the Table 6.1 and prepare a consolidated note on your actions, emotions and lessons learnt.

CHAPTER VII

Men and Machines : Co-Existence

Abstract

After the introduction of automated quotation systems at the exchanges, individual and institutional traders started adopting automated trading systems at their end. Over a period of time, the trading systems have evolved. Artificial Intelligence has been slowly becoming integral part of such systems. It is interesting to see how both human traders and AI based traders compete and collaborate.

Keywords

Automated Trading System, Trading Rules, Artificial Intelligence, Supervised Learning, Unsupervised Learning, Emotions, Ethics

1. Machines March into Markets

> *The men on the trading floor may not have been to school, but they have Ph.D.s in man's ignorance*
> — Michael M. Lewis

Figure 7.1 Can You Guess When and Where

If you knew how stock exchanges were functioning in the 1970s you would have guessed that the photo in Figure 7.1 was taken at the closing time on the trading floor of a stock exchange. To be precise it was at the New York Stock Exchange on March 11, 1976. The scene would have been no different at any stock exchange across the globe from Tokyo to Hong Kong to Bombay to London.

For a first time visitor to a trading floor those days, it would have been all madness. The shouts and yells of the men in suits would have sounded unintelligible gibberish. Whereas the true picture was different. Trading floor was the meeting platform for all those intelligent brokers standing face to face around benches, exchanging bid and offer prices in the language very well understood by them.

Big Bang (1986)

The scene changed after October 1986 when the London Stock Exchange Automated Quotation System replaced the trading floor at the London Stock Exchange. Thereafter there was no need for face to face meetings. There was no need to shout and listen quotes. That was a Big Bang moment in stock trading.

The new platform shortened the period between a trade being initiated and completed. The Big Bang further brought significant benefits to both institutional and individual investors. The individual investors gained low-cost independent access to the market through the new services.

Cheap and efficient trading is what traders wanted and that is what they got. Volumes transacted saw unprecedented growth, with the average daily number of trades going through the ceiling. Machines moved into markets and displaced the suited brokers from trading floors. The conventional trading floor became a thing of the past as electronically-generated trading volumes rose unabated.

Just before the Big Bang's meteoric impact, the average number of daily trades at the London Stock Exchange was 20,000, amounting to about British £700 million worth of shares changing hands. After just one month of the introduction of the automated quotation system, the figure went up to a daily average of 59,000 trades.

In 1987, the London Stock Exchange was transacting as much business in a month as it did in the whole of the previous year, 1986. The average daily value reached British £ 1 billion. These figures would have been impossible to reach without technology.

Large scale automation in the stock exchanges and its resultant efficiency in speed and volume, needed traders and investors to improve their individual systems. They had to design and implement automation of their trading systems with appropriate algorithms.

2. Automated Trading Systems

Whether we are based on carbon or on silicon makes no fundamental difference; we should each be treated with appropriate respect
— Arthur C. Clarke

While the automated quotation system was a big bang moment in stock exchanges, automated trading system was a similar moment for traders and investors. Automated trading systems allow traders to establish specific rules for both trade entries and exits that, once programmed, can be automatically executed via a computer. In fact, it is estimated in 2020 that 80% or even more of shares traded on U.S. stock exchanges come from automated trading systems.

Traders and investors can turn precise entry, exit, and money management rules into automated trading systems that allow computers to execute and monitor trades. One of the biggest attractions is that trades are automatically placed if and when certain criteria are met. There are no emotions coming in the way.

The trade entry and exit rules can be based on simple conditions such as a moving average breaching a threshold. They can even be even more complicated strategies specific to the user, which may require understanding of algorithms and programming languages.

Trading Rules

Some trading platforms have strategy-building wizards that allow users to make selections from a list of commonly available technical indicators to build a set of rules. For example, the user could

- Use the platform's default options
- Input the type of order like market, limit, open or close to trigger a transaction
- Set a rule that a long position trade will be entered once the 50-day moving average crosses above the 200-day moving average on a five-minute chart of a particular trading instrument

Many traders, however, choose to program their own custom indicators and strategies. They will often work closely with the programmer to develop the system. While this typically requires more effort than using the platform's wizard, it allows a much greater degree of flexibility, and the results can be more rewarding.

Once the rules have been established, the computer can monitor the markets to find buy or sell opportunities based on the trading strategy's specifications. Depending on the specific rules, as soon as a trade is entered, any orders for protective stop losses, trailing stops and profit targets will be automatically generated. In fast-moving markets, this instantaneous order entry can mean the difference between a small loss and a catastrophic loss in the event the trade moves against the trader.

Advantages

There is a long list of advantages of automated trading system, of which we present a few.

a) Preserving Discipline

Because trade rules are established and trade execution is performed automatically, discipline is preserved even in volatile markets. Discipline is often lost due to emotional factors such as the fear of taking a loss, or the greed to eke out a little more profit from a trade. Automated trading helps ensure discipline is maintained because machines follow the trading plan exactly.

b) Minimizing Errors

An order to buy 100 shares will not be incorrectly entered as an order to sell 1,000 shares.

c) Retaining Confidence

One of the biggest challenges in trading is to *plan the trade and trade the plan.* There is no trading plan that can win all the time. After all, losses are a part of the game. But losses can be psychologically traumatizing and a trader who has two or three losing trades in a row might decide to skip the next trade. The next trade could be a winner, but the trader has lost confidence and would miss the opportunity. Automated trading systems have no confidence issues. They continue trading the plan.

d) Improving Speed

Since computers respond immediately to changing market conditions, automated trading systems are able to generate orders as soon as trade criteria are met. Getting in or out of a trade a few seconds earlier can make a big difference in the trade's outcome. As soon as a position is entered, all other orders are automatically generated, including protective stop losses and profit targets. Markets can move quickly, and it is demoralizing to have a trade reach the profit target or blow past a stop-loss level before the orders can even be entered. An automated trading system prevents from happening this.

e) Diversifying Trading

Automated trading systems permit the user to trade multiple accounts or various strategies at one time. This has the potential to diversify risk over various instruments while creating a hedge against losing positions. What would be incredibly challenging for a human to accomplish is efficiently executed by a machine in milliseconds. The machine is able to scan for trading opportunities across a range of markets, generate orders and monitor trades.

f) Back Testing

Back testing applies trading rules to historical market data to determine the viability of the idea. When designing a system for automated trading, all rules need to be absolute, with no room for interpretation. The machine cannot make guesses and it has to be told exactly what to do. Traders can take these precise sets of rules and test them on historical data before risking money in live trading. Careful back testing allows to evaluate the return and risk of an idea and fine tune it.

3. Artificial Intelligence

> *AI is the most important thing humanity has ever worked on I think of it as more profound than electricity or fire*
> - Sundar Pichai

Automated trading has the following disadvantages:

- Difficult to write and maintain rules
- Rules are fixed and don't learn from events / mistakes

It is because of such limitations that there is a need to move from mechanical rule based trading to an intelligent self-learning based trading. Intelligent self-learning systems come under the umbrella of Artificial Intelligence (AI).

Before we attempt to look at AI based trading, let us first understand what AI is all about. To do so, let us look at the evolution of AI over the past few decades. Alan Turing came up with what was then known as Imitation Game, now popularly called the Turning's Test. According to the test, a machine is considered to be intelligent if it can fool a human investigator to believe it to be a human, by answering questions at par with a human.

Since the test was proposed, AI research was centered around building machines that not only think like humans but also look like humans. Through the next few decades, the research was focused on enhancing the natural language capability of machines and the hardware for it. Towards the end of the 20th century, AI focus switched back to the mathematics behind it, including the use of Probability, Bayesian Inference and Artificial Neural Networks.

The beginning of the 21st century which marks the advent of Big Data, can be viewed as a major turning point for AI research. With the availability of faster processors, using Machine Learning to achieve Artificial Intelligence started looking feasible. The ability of machines to work with billions of data points at very high speeds led to the wide use of intelligent assistants on our phones. An autonomous vehicle on the road is almost a reality now.

The evolution of AI shows that our notion of artificial intelligence changes as we attain each goal. A smartphone from the 2020s holds more intelligence compared to a PC from the 1990s. With Deep Blue defeating Gary Kasparov in Chess in 1997 and AlphaGo defeating Lee Sedol in Go in

2016, algorithms for intelligent games are no longer major milestones in AI research.

Applied AI

In general, AI research attempts to focus on either Strong AI or Applied AI. Strong AI aims to build machines that think. The ultimate ambition of strong AI is to produce a machine whose overall intellectual ability is indistinguishable from that of a human being; a machine that passes Turing's test. This goal generated great interest in the 1950s and 1960s, but such optimism has given way to an appreciation of the extreme difficulties involved. To date, progress has been meagre.

Applied AI, on the other hand, aims to produce commercially viable smart systems in specific areas. Expert medical diagnosis systems and stock-trading systems are examples of applied AI. Applied AI has been enjoying considerable success.

Our focus in the next section is on applied AI, and that too specifically on stock trading systems. But to do that, we should understand how a machine learns. Like human beings, machines also can learn with or without supervision. And possibly also under semi-supervision.

Supervised learning

As the name indicates, the learning takes place in the presence of a supervisor as a teacher. Let us understand the process through an example. Suppose the machine has to learn the names of the fruits in the Figure 7.2.

Figure 7.2 Apples, Bananas, Grapes, Lemons and Pears

The supervisor explains the features of each fruit and names it, as indicated below:

- If the shape of the object is rounded, has a depression at the top and is red in colour, then it is apple

- If the shape of the object is a long curving cylinder having green-yellow colour, then it is banana
- Similarly describe the features and name other fruits like grape, pear, lemon and so on

The data on features of fruits and the associated names, called labels, is called training data. The training data is essentially labelled. The machine is trained with the help of labelled data.

After training, the machine is subjected to testing. The machine is provided with a new set of examples, called test data, so that the machine applies the learning it has from the training data and produces the correct outcome from the test data.

In our example of fruits, the machine has already learned to recognize each fruit from the training data. If it is presented with a fruit from market, say banana, it will first study the features of the fruit like shape and colour. Based on the features, it classifies the fruit name as banana and puts it in the banana category. Thus, the machine learns from from training data (fruits in Figure 7.2) and then applies the knowledge to the test data (new fruits).

Supervised learning is classified into two categories – Classification and Regression. In the case of classification, the input variable is assigned a category like a banana among fruits. In the case of regression, output variable is derived from the input variables like agricultural production from factors like rainfall.

Unsupervised learning

In contrast to supervised learning where a machine learns with the help of data with labels, in the case of unsupervised learning machine learns from unlabelled data. The machine learns from the given data on its own without any guidance from a supervisor or a teacher.

Here the task of the machine is to group the data based on similarities, and differences. The machine has to find hidden patterns in the data on its own. Let us consider an example. The machine has to identify cats and dogs from the Figure 7.3.

Figure 7.3 Dogs and Cats

Assume that the machine does not know a dog or a cat so far. It has no idea about the features of dogs and cats. There is no teacher to explain the features and name them as dog or cat. But it can categorize them according to their similarities and differences. It can discover patterns that discriminate between dogs and cats. It can categorize the picture into two parts. The first part containing dogs and the second part containing cats.

Unsupervised learning is classified into two categories – Clustering and Association. In clustering, the machine discovers the inherent categories, called clusters, like cats and dogs. In the case of association, the machine discovers rules that describe a portion of the data with the help of other portions of data, like customer behaviour from demographic characteristics.

4. AI Based Trading Systems

The question of whether a computer can think is no more interesting than the question of whether a submarine can swim
— Edsger W. Dijkstra

With reasonably high success rate of applied AI, the future of trading is expected to be shaped by application of AI in trading systems. The expectations from AI based trading are high, including the following:

- examine millions of data points
- analyze markets more accurately
- execute transactions at the best price
- deliver better risk adjusted return

The major advantage of the use of AI is its ability to look at historical data and identify trends in stock prices and returns that might repeat themselves. AI can come out with patterns which would be impossible for the human brain to dig into, in view of the sheer volume of data. Using the patterns, AI based systems can come up with trading strategies, improvise and execute them.

The advantage of AI based trading is that it is emotionless as AI is not designed to have emotions!

Self-Assessment

Adoption of AI based trading needs the following points for consideration:

a) Cost of developing / implementing / improvising / upgrading
b) Trust you can repose into the black box traders
c) Matching your goals with those of AI
d) Loss of skill of understanding markets and theories

Reflect on each of the points and prepare a case for adoption or non-adoption of such trading.

5. AI and Emotions

Pity those who don't feel anything at all
— Sarah J. Maas

Humans are bestowed not only with intelligence and creativity but also with moods and emotions. In our earlier chapters, we highlighted how emotions can help humans achieve what they would otherwise not be able to achieve. We also saw how negative emotions can impede unbiased judgment and hamper rational decision making. Humans quite often make mistakes because of their emotions.

But in the world of machines, there are no emotions. Machines are programmed to rely solely on built-in logic. Trading machines feel no emotions throughout the trading process. By keeping emotions in check, they stick to the plan. They don't hesitate or hasten due to emotions like desire or fear. They don't deviate from logic; they remain stoic and strong.

With the introduction of AI based trading systems, there will be two kinds of traders in the market – human traders and AI based machine traders.

Human traders can understand the behaviour of other human traders and factor emotions of others into their trades. All said and done emotions make human traders vulnerable. With AI based machine traders in the market, human traders have to reckon with emotionless and ruthless machine traders.

Now look at the situation from AI based machine traders' point of view. AI is built based on several theories and models, which assume rational behaviour of participants and markets. But suddenly AI machines encounter irrational decisions from human traders. As AI machines are designed to learn, it is possible that they understand these irrationalities and trade taking into account the vulnerabilities of human traders. It is anybody's guess when and how smoothly it happens.

In any case it is interesting to observe a market with rational AI based machine traders on one side and the emotional yet highly creative human traders on the other side.

Self-Assessment

Think of a situation where there are only AI based machine traders. They all learn from the same set of data using similar algorithms. Over a very short span of time, all machines must be equally informed and equally intelligent. It is expected that they all have same perception of market. When all AI based machine traders have same perception, how does the market function? With no different perceptions of the market, who will buy and who will sell?

We are not sure how such a market functions! Can you visualize?

6. AI and Ethics

*Educating the mind without educating
the heart is no education at all*
— Aristotle

Example 7.1

Imagine you are driving your car at 100 miles per hour from Denali National Park to Fairbanks in Alaska, USA. It is late in the evening and the visibility is already low. There are vehicles ahead of and behind you. As you keep speeding through the road, you suddenly see a fawn coming from one side of the road. The unexpected appearance of the fawn confuses you. You are shocked. Your friend next to you is shouting animatedly.

At the speed you are driving and the very short distance between you and the fawn, you have the following options:

   a) Brake suddenly to save the fawn; with a high possibility of the cars behind you ramming into your car, the intensity of such ramming could be fatal.
   b) Suddenly steer the car to further right avoiding the fawn; with almost a certain risk

of your car getting damaged by hitting the trees and you may escape death by a whisker
c) Steeply steer the car to the left and hit the car coming from opposite side; your car may manage to be safe; opposite driver is likely to be hit and die.
d) Neither brake nor steer away; hit the fawn to death and speed away

Option a) : Fawn survives, car drivers behind you are at moderate risk; you are at moderate risk

Option b) : Fawn survives; car drivers behind you survive; you are at high risk

Option c) : Fawn survives; car driver opposite is at a high risk, you are at moderate risk

Option d) : Fawn gets killed; other drivers have no risk; you have little risk

From the overall risk point of view, option (d) is advisable. But will you choose (d)?

Self-Assessment

When you have the luxury of time to debate the pros and cons of your action, you can rely completely on rational thinking. But in the situation described above, with hardly any time available to you, especially when your friend is yelling - the challenge is how to react and decide. What does your decision making process depend on?

a) Your personality trait
b) Your friend's advice
c) Your ethical values
d) No idea what your action depends on

Ethical Dilemmas of AI

Now let us look at how machines react in such situations. A strictly rational AI based car would act as per option (d). No issues on the importance of life of a fawn. No questions on why human life is to be given more importance than that of a fawn. No emotional factors! No ethical dilemmas!!

Are machines really emotionless? Let us see the process of learning by a machine. It learns from the data it is fed with. If the AI based trading machine learns from greed centric data, the machine is bound to learn the methods of greedy trading. It may not feel greed as it is not designed to feel. But its approach to trading and its strategies may appear similar to the trading of a greedy human trader. The machine may not feel the emotion, greed. It may not know that it is behaving like a greedy human. Still its action may be similar to that of a greedy human.

Similarly, it may acquire trading strategies that are based on emotions like fear, attachment and envy and adopt them.

Though we start with the premise that machines trade without emotions by their original design, they may acquire and adopt methods derived from emotions through their learning process.

Greedy trait in AI based trading machines raises the following ethical questions.

- Is greed a virtue or vice in the case of AI based trading machines?
- Should AI based trading be designed to think only rationally?
- Or should they be allowed to acquire thinking similar to that of greedy human traders?

We leave you with questions to ponder over!

7. Can you Beat an AI Based Trader?

> *We live in a world where machines are playing bigger and bigger roles. Whether you like it or not, it's happening*
> - Gary Kasparov

Consider Usain Bolt running a 100 meters race. Video analytics reveal that he normally attains his highest velocity around 50 to 60 meters into the race. At that point, he runs at about 44 kilometers per hour. Phenomenal speed for a human. But how does it compare with any mean speeding machine. Even in the 1920s there were motor cycles zooming at 160 kilometers per hour; and today they touch as high as 600 kilometers per hour. No human can match that speed.

If you look at lathes, cranes and engines, all created by humans, they can carry and pull loads unimaginable to any human.

In general, machines excel humans in physical work. Do they surpass humans in intelligence? The question is getting a positive response over the past few years.

No human, not even the great *Sakuntala Devi*, the arithmetic wizard of twentieth century from *India*, can match the speed with which large numbers are crunched by machines. The numbers which humans can't even visualize in view of the sheer size, are routinely manipulated by the computers. No fatigue. No errors. No delays.

Arguably considered the greatest chess technician of all times, *Gary Kasparov* had to eventually lose to the brute power of a machine in 1997. DeepBlue could look ahead several moves, which would be impossible for any human. DeepBlue bet *Kasparov*. A stage has come where humans might lose not only by moves but also by clock to the machines, thanks to the phenomenal speed and accuracy the machines are capable of.

As per the recorded registers, a team in Switzerland obtained the value of Pi up to 31.4 trillion digits using high end computers. Arithmetic, which characterized the intelligence of a human for hundreds of years, is now a child's play to a computer; a highly accomplished human stands no chance to be anywhere near a machine.

Medical diagnosis, which is the core of health system, has always been relying on the expertise of knowledgeable physicians. With expert medical systems improving by leaps and bounds, the AI doctor is not only able to diagnose the sickness of a human but also prescribe medicines and do surgeries.

So, whatever was considered a forte of humans, has slowly been taken over by machines; machines surpassing humans in speed, accuracy and precision.

Even arts are no exception. Machines can generate wonderful pieces of art. They can compose pleasing tunes. And they can dabble with literature too.

Can we beat AI based trading machines, is the moot question. Even today AI based trading machines are doing very well in terms of return and risk. It is expected that as years roll by, the difference between AI based machine traders and human traders would increase exponentially leaving human traders way behind.

Does it mean there would not be any human traders? It is very difficult to look into future. We can at best look at the past to guess the future.

Even though there are machines which can beat any chess champion hands down, there are chess competitions and championship events. Though human is no match to any machine in running, Olympics and other tournaments are held to applaud the fastest human runner. Humans still compete with each other for honours.

But stock markets are different. Traders do not play for prize or pride. They play for returns. And when you know that your opponent is a machine, capable of scanning the global events in less than a millisecond, analyze the information and apply techniques like deep learning in its strategies, do you want to play with it against all odds?

We leave this question to you to reflect upon!

8. Looking into the Future

*Machine men, with machine
minds and machine hearts!
You are not machines, you are men!
You have the love of humanity in
your hearts. You don't hate:
Only the unloved hate, the unloved
and the unnatural.
You the people have the power, the
power to create machines,
The power to create happiness! Use that power.*
— Charles Chaplin

What is the future of AI? Certainly there would be powerful and fast computing and communicating systems dominating the world. They will not only dominate your physical activities, but they will also influence your thoughts. Even today, we may not think on our own and decide what we want to eat, drink, wear and travel. Though we may think we are doing all by ourselves.

We are all dictated by our smart gadgets. Unfortunately, many of us are not even aware that we are becoming slaves to the worldwide web which weaves our thoughts and actions.

Unconsciously, we started living like machines, with little freedom of thought and independence of action. We may not be doing so knowingly; it may be happening unknowingly. We follow the smart gadgets, their timings, their advices without even being aware that we are following them. We may be losing our faculty of thinking as we leave it to the man-made intelligent machines. It is possible that the unused brain over a period of time may become dull and dumb.

You may object to our presentation of a gloomy picture of ourselves. You may argue that none of the machines humans invented so far could enslave men. Humans always remained supreme and never became redundant. It did not happen with industrial revolution. It did not happen with large scale computerization. It will not happen with AI.

We can't disagree with you. For two reasons. First. Humans have found ways to tame the machines they invented. None of them became unmanageable Frankensteins. The second reason why we don't disagree with you is the ability of humans to feel. Machines cannot feel. Humans have the unique ability to feel love, affection, sympathy and empathy. Machines can be ruthlessly logical, analytical and rational. They may even *know* the emotions like love, but they cannot *feel* the emotions. So far no AI machine is designed to have such finer feelings.

Humans can be kind to one another. Humans can be considerate to each other. These emotions of love, kindness, empathy and consideration, we strongly feel, will help humans to cope with the machines even when the machines are more intelligent.

Self-Test 7.1

Look at the score from the finals between Nadal and Medvedev at Australian Open 2022, given in the Figure 7.4. Nadal was down two sets and trailing 2-3 in third set with 0-40 score. From the score board you can see Medvedev was seeded 2 compared to Nadal's seeding of 6. You also know that Nadal just recovered from a foot surgery in September 2021.

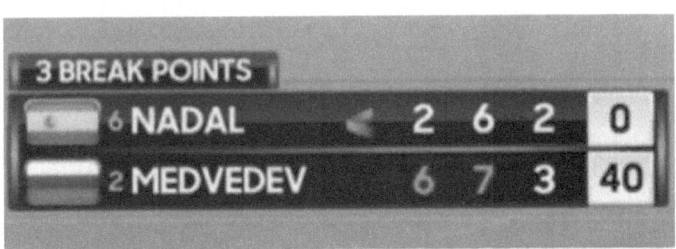

Figure 7.4 Australian Open 2022 Finals Scorecard

Suppose you were asked to estimate the chances of winning of Nadal and Medvedev. What will be your estimate?

a) 95 % to Medvedev 5 % to Nadal
b) 50% to Medvedev 50% to Nadal
c) 5% to Medvedev 95% to Nadal

You can write down reasons for your choice.

Self-Test 7.2

Let us see what AI engines predicted at that stage. AI surely would have analyzed the present position appearing on scoreboard. Further it would have factored all the information from the large volumes of data on individual players, their styles, previous victory statistics, type of courts and so on. They would also have done video analytics of individual body language, fatigue, frustration, determination and so on. If AI did not do all this, we feel that it is no AI worth the salt.

After all this deep dive, which AI is capable of doing very quickly and efficiently, it gave 96% chance to Medvedev and 4% chance to Nadal, at that juncture.

If you were sitting in the Melbourne stadium as a Nadal fan, what would you have thought? Forget AI. Forget predictions. Nadal would win! Your love and affection would make you believe that Nadal would win under any circumstances. Your emotions overtake your logic. Not only yours. The entire crowd in Melbourne stadium was cheering Nadal to win.

What happened? Nadal's emotions pushed him. Though his body was weak (which was evident when he asked for a chair to sit during the prize ceremony later) he rose to the occasion. He fought like an unbeatable force. He ran, dived, and played all shots in his armour. By sheer emotional strength he bet Medvedev 2-6, 6-7, 6-4, 6-4, 7-5!

How can AI predict the strength of emotions, which a human alone is capable of? It failed to recognize the strength of Nadal's emotion and naturally, it failed in its prediction.

Machines, whose intelligence is designed on the lines of a human brain and nervous system, cannot go beyond the logic they are endowed with. They may be fast. They may be strong. Yet they remain subservient to their masters. They cannot make humans their slaves until and unless humans decide on their own to become slaves to machines.

It is a matter of time when intelligent humans and intelligent machines co-exist. They learn to manage each other. Stock markets will be no different. Human traders and AI based traders co-exist. At least for some more time to come. Thereafter, if humans find it convenient to use only AI based traders, then there would only be AI based traders. But if the gambler in humans want to take over trading any point of time, no AI based trader can stop.

There have been several instances in the history of civilization when human heuristic hunches worked better. Weird and quixotic ideas opened up new vistas. Human intelligence is limitless whereas AI is limited by the boundaries set to it by humans themselves.

One last interesting question that nags us – will AI machines ever have emotions? In other words, will humans ever enable AI machines the ability to feel? Or more correctly, can humans ever create emotional AI machines?

CHAPTER VIII
Lessons Learnt and Way Forward

We trust our book helped you to learn -

*Influence of your emotions
on your decisions
Assessment of your emotional traits
Probability Theory in the
World of Uncertainty
Stock Market Theories
Recent Developments in
Behavioural Finance
Influence of Emotions on Market Crashes
Playing with Emotionless Machines*

As a way forward -

*Take decisions only when you are
free from negative emotions
Use all information from markets
and knowledge from theories
Even after all this, be prepared
for any kind of outcome*

Our final advice -

*Like you work on your health
and wealth during good days
to serve you as useful
resources when needed*

*Learn to deal with your negative
emotions during good times
to reduce their effect on your
decisions when needed*

Recommended Reading

Emotions

DeSteno, David. (2018) *Emotioinal Success*, Houghton Mifflin Harcourt

Gilbert, Daniel. (2007) *Stumbling on Happiness*, Knopf

James, William. (1890) *Principles of Psychology*, Henry Holt and Company

Ramasastri, AS. (2011) *Irrational Behaviour and Beautiful Faces*, Business Standard

Smith, Tiffany. (2016) *The Book of Human Emotions*, Profile Books Limited

Investing

Bogle, John. (2017) *Common Sense of Investing*, Wiley

Dorsey, Pat. (2004) *The Five Rules for Successful Stock Investing*, Wiley

Graham, Benjamin. (2003) *The Intelligent Investor*, Harper

Kratter, Mathew. (2019) *A Beginner's Guide to Stock Market*, Trader University

Murnighan, Keith and Mowen, John. (2002) *The Art of High-Stakes Decision-Making*, Wiley

Probability

Bertsekas, Dimitri and Tsitsiklis, John. (2008) *Introduction to Probability*, Athena Scientific

Chung, Kai Lai. (2007) *Elementary Probability Theory*, Springer

Hacking, Ian. (2001) *An Introduction to Probability and Inductive Logic*, Cambridge University Press

Resnic, Sidney. (2002) *Adventures in Stochastic Processes*, Springer

Sheldon, Ross. (2013) *A First Course of Probability*, Pearson

Finance

Bernstein, Peter. (2005) *Capital Ideas: The Improbable Origins of Modern Wall Street*, Wiley

Heilbroner, Robert. (1953) *The Worldly Philosophers*, Touchstone

Helfert, Erich. (2003) *Techniques of Financial Analysis*, McGraw-Hill

Merton, Robert. (1990) *Continuous-Time Finance*, Wiley

Sharpe, William, Alexander, Gordon and Bailey, Jeffery. (1995) *Investments*, Prentice-Hall

Behavioural Finance

Ariely, Dan. (2010) *The Upside of Irrationality*, Harper

Kahneman, Daniel. (2011) *Thinking Fast and Slow*, Allen Lane

Malkiel, Burton. (1973) *A Random Walk Down Wall Street*, Norton

Taleb, Nassim Nicholas. (2007) *The Black Swan*, Penguin

Weatherall, James Owen. (2013) *The Physics of Wall Street*, Houghton Mifflin Harcourt

Artificial Intelligence

Bostrom, Nick. (2016) *Superintelligence: Paths, Dangers, and Strategies*, Oxford University Press

Kurzweil, Ray. (2013) *How to Create a Mind*, Penguin

Lee, Kai-Fu. (2021) *AI 2041*, WH Allen

Russell, Stuart and Norvig, Peter. (2019) *Artificial Intelligence*, Pearson

Tegmark, Max. (2017) *Life 3.0 Being Human in the Age of Artificial Intelligence,* Knopf

www.ingramcontent.com/pod-product-compliance
Lightning Source LLC
Chambersburg PA
CBHW020727180526
45163CB00001B/142